TALK TO ME IN KOREAN
LEVEL 2

Conjunctions, Tenses, Telling Time,
and More

This book is based on a series of published lessons, divided into ten levels, which are currently available at https://talktomeinkorean.com.

Talk To Me In Korean - Level 2

I판 I쇄 • 1st edition published	2015. II. 16.	
I판 I9쇄 • 19th edition published	2024. IO. 2I.	

지은이 • Written by	Talk To Me In Korean
책임편집 • Edited by	선경화 Kyung-hwa Sun, 스테파니 베이츠 Stephanie Bates
디자인 • Designed by	선윤아 Yoona Sun
삽화 • Illustrations by	김경해 Kyounghae Kim
녹음 • Voice Recordings by	선현우 Hyunwoo Sun, 최경은 Kyeong-eun Choi
펴낸곳 • Published by	롱테일북스 Longtail Books
펴낸이 • Publisher	이수영 Su Young Lee
편집 • Copy-edited by	김보경 Florence Kim
주소 • Address	04033 서울특별시 마포구 양화로 II3, 3층(서교동, 순흥빌딩)
	3rd Floor, II3 Yanghwa-ro, Mapo-gu, Seoul, KOREA
이메일 • E-mail	TTMIK@longtailbooks.co.kr
ISBN	979-II-86701-08-9 I4710

*이 교재의 내용을 사전 허가 없이 전재하거나 복제할 경우 법적인 제재를 받게 됨을 알려 드립니다.

*잘못된 책은 구입하신 서점이나 본사에서 교환해 드립니다.

*정가는 표지에 표시되어 있습니다.

TTMIK - TALK TO ME IN KOREAN

MESSAGE
FROM
THE AUTHOR

Welcome to Level 2 of the Talk To Me In Korean book series! Whether you have already studied with the Level 1 book, or you have chosen this book because it is the right level for you, we hope that you enjoy learning Korean with us.

When learning a new language, especially if embarking on a self-study journey, it is very important to find a variety of ways to help improve your listening, speaking, reading, and writing skills. We strongly recommend seeking out other resources to help with your language study. There is a workbook available to accompany this book in addition to free MP3 audio files to download and take with you wherever you go. We, and a community of Korean learners just like you, are always available on your favorite social media network to help you practice.

After studying with this book, you will be able to hold simple conversations in Korean and have an expanded vocabulary. Level 1 and Level 2 introduce the most essential sentence structures, grammar points, tenses, and vocabulary which give you the strong foundation you need to take your Korean language skills even further through subsequent lessons and practice.

Thank you for giving us your support and for studying with Talk To Me In Korean. Good luck with your studies, and enjoy Level 2!

TABLE OF
CONTENTS

LESSON **1**

Future Tense

```
-(으)ㄹ 거예요
```

Welcome to Level 2 and congratulations on making it through Level 1!

In Level 2, you will build upon what was learned in Level 1 with new grammar points and expressions.

Let's get started with the first lesson where you will learn how to use the sentence ending expressing the future in Korean.

Future Tense

The most common way of making future tense sentences in Korean is by adding

-(으)ㄹ 거예요.

[-(eu)l kkeo-ye-yo]

> ### *Conjugation*
>
> Verb + -(으)ㄹ 거예요 = future tense

Conjunctions, Tenses,

Determining whether to use -ㄹ 거예요 or -을 거예요:

1. Verb stems ending with a vowel (보다, 가다, 자다) are followed by -ㄹ 거예요.

보다 + -ㄹ/을 거예요 = 볼 거예요.
[bo-da]   [bol kkeo-ye-yo.]
가다 + -ㄹ/을 거예요 = 갈 거예요.
[ga-da]   [gal kkeo-ye-yo.]
자다 + -ㄹ/을 거예요 = 잘 거예요.
[ja-da]   [jal kkeo-ye-yo.]

2. Verb stems ending with a consonant (먹다, 찾다, 붙다) are followed by -을 거예요.

먹다 + -ㄹ/을 거예요 = 먹을 거예요.
[meok-tta]   [meo-geul kkeo-ye-yo.]
찾다 + -ㄹ/을 거예요 = 찾을 거예요.
[chat-tta]   [cha-jeul kkeo-ye-yo.]
붙다 + -ㄹ/을 거예요 = 붙을 거예요.
[but-tta]   [bu-teul kkeo-ye-yo.]

(*There is no complex reason for this. It is simply for the ease of pronunciation.*)

Track 01

3. Exception: Verb stems already ending with ㄹ (놀다, 멀다, 살다) are followed only by 거예요.

놀다 + -ㄹ/을 거예요 = 놀 거예요.
[nol-da]   [nol kkeo-ye-yo.]
멀다 + -ㄹ/을 거예요 = 멀 거예요.
[meol-da]   [meol kkeo-ye-yo.]
살다 + -ㄹ/을 거예요 = 살 거예요.
[sal-da]   [sal kkeo-ye-yo.]

When a verb is changed into this form, it takes on the meaning of "to be going to" do something or "will" do something, but as you will find out when you hear more conversations between native speakers, the present tense can also serve to express the future when the context is very clear.

For example, "I am going to go tomorrow" is "내일 갈 거예요" in the future tense, but "내일
                                                      [nae-il]
가요" (which is in the present tense) may still make perfect sense depending on the situation.

9

1. 가다 = to go   가 + ㄹ 거예요.

  → 갈 거예요. = I am going to go. / I will go.

  Ex)

  지금 갈 거예요. = I am going to go (there) now.
  [ji-geum]
  혼자 갈 거예요. = I am going to go alone.
  [hon-ja]
  내일 갈 거예요. = I am going to go tomorrow.

2. 하다 = to do   하 + ㄹ 거예요.
   [ha-da]
  → 할 거예요. = I am going to do (it). / I will do (it).
   [hal kkeo-ye-yo.]

  Ex)

  뭐 할 거예요? = What are you going to do?
  [mwo]
  언제 할 거예요? = When are you going to do (it)?
  [eon-je]
  이거 언제 할 거예요? = When are you going to do this?
  [i-geo eon-je]
  이거 정말 할 거예요? = Are you really going to do it?
  [i-geo jeong-mal]

3. 입다 = to wear   입 + 을 거예요.
   [ip-tta]
  → 입을 거예요. = I am going to wear (it). / I will wear (it).
   [i-beul kkeo-ye-yo.]

  Ex)

  청바지 입을 거예요. = I am going to wear blue jeans.
  [cheong-ba-ji]
  뭐 입을 거예요? = What are you going to wear?
  [mwo]
  티셔츠 입을 거예요. = I am going to wear a t-shirt.
  [ti-syeo-cheu]
  치마 입을 거예요. = I am going to wear a skirt.
  [chi-ma]

4. 만나다 = to meet   만나 + ㄹ 거예요.
[man-na-da]
→ 만날 거예요. = I am going to meet (him/her/that person/them). / I will meet (him/
[man-nal kkeo-ye-yo.]
her/that person/them).

Ex)

누구 만날 거예요? = Who are you going to meet?
[nu-gu]
어디에서 만날 거예요? = Where are you going to meet?
[eo-di-e-seo]
언제 만날 거예요? = When are you going to meet?

5. 팔다 = to sell   팔 + 거예요.
[pal-da]
→ 팔 거예요. = I am going to sell (it). / I will sell (it).
[pal kkeo-ye-yo.]

Ex)

**Track
01**

뭐 팔 거예요? = What are you going to sell?

어디에서 팔 거예요? = Where are you going to sell it?

얼마에 팔 거예요? = At what price are you going to sell it?
[eol-ma-e]

Sample Dialogue

Track
02

A: 밥 언제 먹을 거예요?
[bap eon-je meo-geul kkeo-ye-yo?]

B: 지금 먹을 거예요.
[ji-geum meo-geul kkeo-ye-yo.]

A: 어디에서 먹을 거예요?
[eo-di-e-seo meo-geul kkeo-ye-yo?]

B: 밖에 나가서 먹을 거예요.
[ba-kke na-ga-seo meo-geul kkeo-ye-yo.]

A: When are you going to eat?

B: I am going to eat now.

A: Where are you going to eat?

B: I am going to go out to eat.

12

✎ Exercises for Lesson 1

Translate the following sentences to Korean:

1. "I am going to wear blue jeans."
   * 입다 = to wear, 청바지 = blue jeans
     [ip-tta]   [cheong-ba-ji]

   ( )

2. "What are you going to sell?"
   * 팔다 = to sell
     [pal-da]

   ( )

3. "Who are you going to meet?"
   * 만나다 = to meet
     [man-na-da]

   ( )

4. "When are you going to eat lunch?"
   * 점심 = lunch, 먹다 = to eat
     [jeom-sim]   [meok-tta]

   ( )

5. "What are you going to do tomorrow?"

   ( )

Check the answers on **p.196**

13

LESSON 2

Object Marking Particles

-을, -를

**Track
03**

In Level 1 Lesson 9, topic marking particles (-은, -는) and subject marking particles (-이, -가)
[-eun] [-neun]   [-i] [-ga]
were introduced. Particles may still be new and different to many people, and it may seem
like an impossible task to truly grasp the function of these particles, but with this lesson,
learning how and when to use object marking particles is broken down to make it easier to
understand.

Object marking particles create a relation to the verb in the sentence. Although quite a
few specific verbs have been introduced previously, in general, verbs can be divided into
transitive (verbs which need a direct object) and intransitive verbs (verbs which do not
require a direct object). This is clearer in English than it is in Korean. Take a look at the
following exchange in English:

> Speaker A: "Did you find your wallet?"
> Speaker B: "Yes, I found it."

14

"Find"/"found" is a transitive verb and needs a DIRECT OBJECT. "Wallet" is the direct object in the first sentence, and "it" (object pronoun) in the second sentence.

In Korean, however, the sentences are as follows:

Speaker A: "지갑 찾았어요?" (Literal translation: "Wallet found?")
[ji-gap cha-ja-sseo-yo?]
Speaker B: "네. 찾았어요." (Literal translation: "Yes. Found.")
[ne. cha-ja-sseo-yo.]

There is no direct object in the second sentence, but Speaker A knows what Speaker B is referring to without it. The distinction between transitive and intransitive is not as strong in Korean as in English or other languages.

How is that possible?!

Track 03

That is where object marking particles come into play.

Object marking particles:

> ### Conjugation
> -을 - used after a noun ending in a consonant
> -를 - used after a noun ending in a vowel

우유(milk) + -를 = 우유를
[u-yu-reul]
책(book) + -을 = 책을
[chae-geul]
모자(hat) + -를 = 모자를
[mo-ja-reul]
카메라(camera) + -를 = 카메라를
[ka-me-ra-reul]
방(room) + -을 = 방을
[bang-eul]

15

So what exactly do particles in Korean do anyway?

To explain it simply, they help listeners/readers predict the verb (to an extent).

In English, if you say or write "an apple", it is simply a noun; a round, shiny, sweet fruit. If you write or say a sentence and do not use a verb to go with it, the reader/listener has no idea what ACTION is directly happening to the apple in the sentence.

Ex)

"Did you _____ an apple?" → The verb can be any action verb: buy, sell, trade, eat, throw, etc. (transitive verb)

Track 03

Likewise, if you say or write just "the apple", the reader/listener has no clue ABOUT the apple. Did the apple DO an action? Is there something about the apple that he/she needs to know?

Ex)

"The apple." → The apple "what"? In this case, either an intransitive verb (rolled, disappeared, fell, emerged, vanished, etc.) or adjective (is good, bad, ugly, pretty, shiny, etc.) can be used to complete the sentence.

In Korean, 사과 is "apple". By adding only -를 (object marking particle), to 사과, making 사과
[sa-gwa]   [-reul]
를, one can predict that 사과 is the direct OBJECT of the verb in the sentence, meaning that the verb's ACTION (transitive verb) will be directly transferred to the 사과.

Ex)

사과를 먹었어요? (Did you eat an apple?)
[sa-gwa-reul meo-geo-sseo-yo?]

16

사과를 사요? (Are you buying an apple?)
[sa-gwa-reul sa-yo?]

By adding -가 (subject marking particle) to 사과, it becomes the SUBJECT of the sentence, meaning that the verb will be ABOUT the 사과 (absolutely NO action is being directly transferred to the 사과). It is easy to predict the verb or adjective (known as a "descriptive verb" in Korean) here as well.

Ex)

이 사과가 맛있어요. (This apple is delicious.)
[i sa-gwa-ga ma-si-sseo-yo.]
사과가 떨어졌어요. (The apple fell.)
[sa-gwa-ga tteo-reo-jyeo-sseo-yo.]

When adding -는 (topic marking particle) to create 사과는, the reader/listener knows that 사과 will be compared to something else, or that 사과 is being brought up in the conversation for the first time. All this without any other words!

Track 03

How particles are dropped

In Korean, particles are sometimes necessary in order to clarify the meaning of a sentence, especially when changing the word order or forming long sentences. Sometimes, however, there are certain situations where particles can be dropped if the meaning of the sentence is clearly understood or for ease of pronunciation and for the sake of shortening the phrase.

Ex)

사과를 사요? → 사과 사요? (Are you buying an apple?)
[sa-gwa-reul sa-yo?]
이 사과가 맛있어요. → 이 사과 맛있어요. (This apple is delicious.)
[i sa-gwa-ga ma-si-sseo-yo.]

The meaning of these sentences stays the same with or without a particle.

"When do I need to use object or subject marking particles?"

You need to use them when you want to clarify the relationship between the object or subject and the verb. When the object or subject is close to the verb, such as in the sentences before, using a particle or omitting it does not make much of a difference since the meaning is still the same. However, when sentences become longer, there are more elements, the word order can change, and the object or subject gets further away from the verb. Using a particle is absolutely necessary in this situation to clarify the meaning.

Sample Sentences

Track 03

만났어요.
[man-na-sseo-yo.]
= I met.

→ 만났어요?

= Did you meet?

→ 누구 만났어요?
[nu-gu]
= Who did you meet?

→ 어제 여기에서 누구(를) 만났어요?
[eo-je yeo-gi-e-seo nu-gu-(reul) man-na-sseo-yo?]
= Who did you meet here yesterday?

→ 어제 누구를 여기에서 만났어요?

= WHO did you meet here yesterday?

텔레비전 봐요.
[tel-le-bi-jeon bwa-yo.]
= I watch TV.

→ 텔레비전 봐요?

= Do you watch TV?

→ 텔레비전 자주 봐요?
[ja-ju]
= Do you watch TV often?

→ 일주일에 몇 번 텔레비전 봐요?
[il-jju-i-re myeot beon]
= How many times per week do you watch TV?

→ 텔레비전(을) 일주일에 몇 번 봐요?
= How many times a week do you watch TV?

Don't worry too much about the other elements of the sentences above for now. Just focus on remembering that the longer the sentence is, the more necessary it is to use particles!

Track 03

19

Sample Dialogue

Track 04

A: 핸드폰을 잃어버렸어요.
[haen-deu-po-neul i-reo-beo-ryeo-sseo-yo.]

B: 어디에서 잃어버렸어요?
[eo-di-e-seo i-reo-beo-ryeo-sseo-yo?]

A: 잘 모르겠어요.
[jal mo-reu-ge-sseo-yo.]

A: I have lost my cell phone.

B: Where did you lose it?

A: I am not sure.

Conjunctions, Tenses,

✏ Exercises for Lesson 2

-을 and -를 *are object marking particles in Korean. Do you remember how to decide which one is used? Please fill in the blanks with either* "-을" *or* "-를".

1. 사과 ( )

2. 핸드폰 ( )
[hean-deu-pon]

3. 공부 ( )
[gong-bu]

4. 시계 ( )
[si-gye]

5. 여행 ( )
[yeo-haeng]

Check the answers on **p.196**

21

LESSON 3

And, And then, Therefore, So

그리고, 그래서

The last two lessons contained fairly heavy topics (future tense and object marking particles), but in this lesson, your brain gets a bit of a break!

Korean has conjunctions (part of speech which connects words, sentences, phrases, or clauses) just like many other languages around the world. There are many of them in Korean, but you will learn two of the most common in this lesson.

그리고

그리고 has the meaning of "and" or "and then" depending on the context. 그리고 can
[geu-ri-go]
be used for both linking nouns and phrases, but in colloquial situations, 그리고 is more commonly used for linking phrases.

> **Ex)** (linking nouns)
> 커피, 빵, 그리고 물 = coffee, bread, and water
> [keo-pi, ppang, geu-ri-go mul]

22

서울 그리고 부산 = Seoul and Busan
[seo-ul geu-ri-go bu-san]

런던 그리고 파리 = London and Paris
[leon-deon geu-ri-go pa-ri]

미국 그리고 호주 = United States and Australia
[mi-guk geu-ri-go ho-ju]

독일 그리고 필리핀 = Germany and the Philippines
[do-gil geu-ri-go pil-li-pin]

Ex) (linking phrases)

(1) 친구를 만났어요.
[chin-gu-reul man-na-sseo-yo.]

친구 = friend

를 = object marking particle

만나다 = to meet
[man-na-da]

만났어요 = past tense of 만나다

(2) 밥을 먹었어요.
[ba-beul meo-geo-sseo-yo.]

밥 = rice, meal
[bap]

을 = object marking particle
[eul]

먹다 = to eat
[meok-tta]

먹었어요 = past tense of 먹다

Track 05

(1) and (2) = 친구를 만났어요 and 밥을 먹었어요.

= 친구를 만났어요. 그리고 밥을 먹었어요.

그래서

그래서 has the meaning of "therefore" and "so", and just as in English, using this word
[geu-rae-seo]
between two sentences shows a logical relation between sentences.

23

Ex)

(1) 오늘은 비가 왔어요.
[o-neu-reun bi-ga wa-sseo-yo.]

비가 오다 = to rain
[o-da]

비가 왔어요 = past tense of 비가 오다

(2) 집에 있었어요.
[ji-be i-sseo-sseo-yo.]

집 = house, home
[jip]

있다 = to be
[it-tta]

있었어요 = past tense of 있다

(1) + (2) = 오늘은 비가 왔어요. Therefore, 집에 있었어요.

= 오늘은 비가 왔어요. 그래서 집에 있었어요.

Track 05

Sample Sentences

김치는 맛있어요. 그리고 한국 음식이에요.
[gim-chi-neun ma-si-sseo-yo. geu-ri-go han-guk eum-si-gi-e-yo.]
= Kimchi is delicious. And it is Korean food.

김치 = kimchi

맛있다 = to be delicious
[ma-sit-tta]

한국 음식 = Korean food
[han-guk eum-sik]

저는 학생이에요. 그리고 프랑스어를 공부해요.
[jeo-neun hak-ssaeng-i-e-yo. geu-ri-go peu-rang-sseu-eo-reul gong-bu-hae-yo.]
= I am a student. And I am studying French.

저 = I (humble)

학생 = student

프랑스어 = French (language)

공부하다 = to study
[gong-bu-ha-da]

24

Conjunctions, Tenses,

저는 학생이에요. 그래서 돈이 없어요.
[jeo-neun hak-ssaeng-i-e-yo. geu-rae-seo do-ni eop-sseo-yo.]
= I am a student. So, I do not have money.

돈 = money

없다 = to not be, to not exist
[eop-tta]

김치는 맛있어요. 그래서 김치를 많이 먹어요.
[gim-chi-neun ma-si-sseo-yo. geu-rae-seo gim-chi-reul ma-ni meo-geo-yo.]
= Kimchi is delicious. So, I eat a lot of kimchi.

많이 = a lot, many (in quantity or frequency)

먹다 = to eat

저는 한국인이에요. 그래서 김치를 많이 먹어요.
[jeo-neun han-gu-gi-ni-e-yo. geu-rae-seo gim-chi-reul ma-ni meo-geo-yo.]
= I am Korean. So, I eat a lot of kimchi.

한국인 = Korean (person)
[han-gu-gin]

Track 05

저는 김치를 많이 먹어요. 그래서 튼튼해요.
[jeo-neun gim-chi-reul ma-ni meo-geo-yo. geu-rae-seo teun-teun-hae-yo.]
= I eat a lot of kimchi. Therefore, I am strong.

튼튼하다 = to be strong
[teun-teun-ha-da]

Sample Dialogue

A: 오늘 많이 아팠어요. 그래서 회사를
못 갔어요.
[o-neul ma-ni a-pa-sseo-yo. geu-rae-seo hoe-sa-reul
mot ga-sseo-yo.]

B: 진짜요? 병원 갔다 왔어요?
[jin-jja-yo? byeong-won gat-tta wa-sseo-yo?]

A: 아니요. 지금 갈 거예요.
[a-ni-yo. ji-geum gal kkeo-ye-yo.]

A: I was very sick today.
Therefore, I could not go to work.

B: Really? Have you been to the
hospital?

A: No. I am going to go now.

26

✏️ Exercises for Lesson *3*

Please fill in the blanks with **"그리고"** *or* **"그래서"**.

1. 책, 연필 (   ) 공책
[chaek, yeon-pil]   [gong-chaek]
= A book, a pencil, and a notebook.

2. 저는 학생이에요. (   ) 돈이 없어요.
[jeo-neun hak-ssaeng-i-e-yo.]   [do-ni eop-sseo-yo.]
= I am a student. Therefore, I do not have money.

3. 김밥은 맛있어요. (   ) 김밥을 자주 먹어요.
[gim-ppa-beun ma-si-sseo-yo.]   [gim-ppa-beul ja-ju meo-geo-yo.]
= Kimbap is delicious. So, I eat kimbap often.

4. 서울 (   ) 부산
[seo-ul]   [bu-san]
= Seoul and Busan

5. 예지 씨는 예뻐요. (   ) 노래도 잘해요.
[ye-ji ssi-neun ye-ppeo-yo.]   [no-rae-do ja-rae-yo.]
= Yeji is pretty. And she also sings well.

Check the answers on **p.196**

27

LESSON 4

And, With

-하고, -(이)랑

Track 07

As mentioned in the previous lesson, there are many conjunctions in Korean, especially when it comes to the word "and". Continue the quest of learning conjunctions in Korean with this lesson on -하고 and -(이)랑.
[-ha-go]   [-(i)-rang]

-하고 = and

Conjugation

-하고 is used like a particle and attached to a noun without space.
[-ha-go]

Ex)

이거
[i-geo]
= this, this thing

이거하고 이거
[i-geo-ha-go i-geo]
= this and this

Conjunctions, Tenses,

이거하고 이거 주세요.
[i-geo-ha-go i-geo ju-se-yo.]
= Give me this and this.

<h2 style="text-align:center">-(이)랑 = and</h2>

Conjugation

If a noun ends in a vowel, attach -랑 at the end, and if it ends with a consonant,
[-rang]

use -이랑. This makes it easier to pronounce.
[-i-rang]

* *-(이)랑 and -하고 are almost always interchangeable, but -(이)랑 is more colloquial and casual,*
and not often used in formal settings.

Track
07

Ex)

우유 = milk
[u-yu]

빵 = bread
[ppang]

우유랑 빵 = milk and bread

빵이랑 우유 = bread and milk

우유하고 빵 = milk and bread

우유랑 빵 샀어요. = I bought milk and bread.
[sa-sseo-yo.]

우유하고 빵 샀어요. = I bought milk and bread.

빵이랑 우유 샀어요. = I bought bread and milk.

Another meaning of -하고 and -(이)랑

Depending on the context of the sentence, both -하고 and -(이)랑 can also mean "with", and it is usually very easy to tell whether it is used as "and" or "with".

친구하고 영화 봤어요.
[chin-gu-ha-go yeong-hwa bwa-sseo-yo.]
= I saw a movie with a friend.*

* It is very unlikely that this sentence means "I watched a friend and a movie".

누구랑 갔어요?
[nu-gu-rang ga-sseo-yo?]
= Who did you go with?

Track 07

To make the meaning of a sentence clearer, add the word 같이 after -하고 or -(이)랑. 같이
[ga-chi]
means "together", so -하고 같이 or -(이)랑 같이 means "together with". While saying "친구하고 영화 봤어요" makes perfect sense, if you say "친구하고 같이 영화 봤어요", it is even better. The same can be said for "누구랑 갔어요?" and "누구랑 같이 갔어요?"

Sample Sentences

동생하고 공부할 거예요.
[dong-saeng-ha-go gong-bu-hal kkeo-ye-yo.]
= 동생이랑 공부할 거예요.
[dong-saeng-i-rang gong-bu-hal kkeo-ye-yo.]
= I am going to study with my younger brother/sister.

선생님하고 밥을 먹을 거예요.
[seon-saeng-ni-ma-go ba-beul meo-geul kkeo-ye-yo.]
= 선생님이랑 밥을 먹을 거예요.
[seon-saeng-ni-mi-rang ba-beul meo-geul kkeo-ye-yo.]
= I am going to eat with my teacher.

30

내일 선생님하고 경복궁에 갈 거예요.
[nae-il seon-saeng-ni-ma-go gyeong-bok-kkung-e gal kkeo-ye-yo.]
= 내일 선생님이랑 경복궁에 갈 거예요.
[nae-il seon-saeng-ni-mi-rang gyeong-bok-kkung-e gal kkeo-ye-yo.]
= I am going to go to Gyeongbok Palace with my teacher tomorrow.

어제 홍대하고 신촌에 갔어요.
[eo-je hong-dae-ha-go sin-cho-ne ga-sseo-yo.]
= 어제 홍대랑 신촌에 갔어요.
[eo-je hong-dae-rang sin-cho-ne ga-sseo-yo.]
= I went to Hongdae and Sinchon yesterday.

* 홍대 *and* 신촌 *are both popular hang out spots in Seoul for younger people.*

Track 07

31

Sample Dialogue

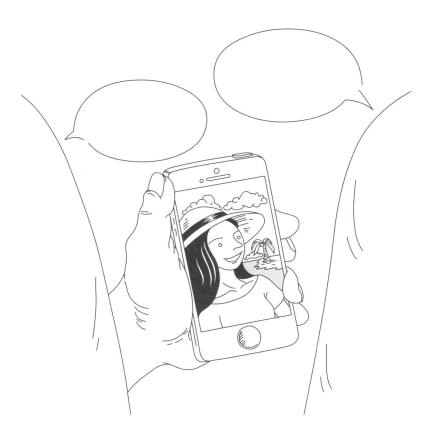

A: 여행 누구랑 갔다 왔어요?
[yeo-haeng nu-gu-rang gat-tta wa-sseo-yo?]

B: 가족들이랑 갔다 왔어요.
[ga-jok-tteu-ri-rang gat-tta wa-sseo-yo.]

A: 어디로 갔다 왔어요?
[eo-di-ro gat-tta wa-sseo-yo?]

B: 보라카이로 갔다 왔어요.
[bo-ra-ka-i-ro gat-tta wa-sseo-yo.]

A: Who did you travel with?

B: I traveled with my family.

A: Where did you go?

B: We went to Boracay.

✎ Exercises for Lesson 4

Fill in the blanks to complete the Korean sentences.

1. 친구(   ) 영화 봤어요.

= I saw a movie with a friend.

2. 누구(   ) 같이 갔어요?

= Who did you go with?

3. 김밥(   ) 라면 좋아해요.
[gim-ppap]   [ra-myeon jo-a-hae-yo.]

= I like kimbap and ramen noodles.

4. 동생(   ) 스케이트장 갈 거예요.
[dong-saeng]   [seu-ke-i-teu-jang gal kkeo-ye-yo.]

= I am going to go ice skating with my younger brother/sister.

5. 노트(   ) 펜 가지고 오세요.
[no-teu]   [pen ga-ji-go o-se-yo.]

= Please bring your notebook and pen.

Check the answers on **p.196**

LESSON 5

Days of the Week

요일

Track 09

After completing this lesson, you will be able to recognize and use the Korean words for each day of the week.

Sunday	Monday	Tuesday	Wednesday	Thursday	Friday	Saturday
일요일	월요일	화요일	수요일	목요일	금요일	토요일
[i-ryo-il]	[wo-ryo-il]	[hwa-yo-il]	[su-yo-il]	[mo-gyo-il]	[geu-myo-il]	[to-yo-il]

The syllables 요 and 일 together mean "day of the week" in Korean. Each day has its own unique first syllable.

Let's glance at the 한자 characters (한자 is the Korean word for Chinese characters) that are used in the names of the days of the week.

Conjunctions, Tenses,

月 = 월 = moon
[wol]

火 = 화 = fire
[hwa]

水 = 수 = water
[su]

木 = 목 = tree
[mok]

金 = 금 = gold, metal, iron
[geum]

土 = 토 = earth, soil, ground
[to]

日 = 일 = sun
[il]

The names for the days of the week can also be related to some of the planets in our solar system.

화요일 = Tuesday / 화성 = Mars
[hwa-seong]

수요일 = Wednesday / 수성 = Mercury
[su-seong]

목요일 = Thursday / 목성 = Jupiter
[mok-sseong]

금요일 = Friday / 금성 = Venus
[geum-seong]

토요일 = Saturday / 토성 = Saturn
[to-seong]

Track 09

Sample Sentences

토요일에는 소풍을 갈 거예요.
[to-yo-i-re-neun so-pung-eul gal kkeo-ye-yo.]
= I am going to go on a picnic on Saturday.

어제는 신나는 금요일이었어요.
[eo-je-neun sin-na-neun geu-myo-i-ri-eo-sseo-yo.]
= Yesterday was an exciting Friday.

저는 월요일에 영화를 봤어요.
[jeo-neun wo-ryo-i-re yeong-hwa-reul bwa-sseo-yo.]
= I watched a movie on Monday.

Sample Dialogue

Track 10

A: 오늘 무슨 요일이에요?
[o-neul mu-seun yo-i-ri-e-yo?]

B: 화요일이에요.
[hwa-yo-i-ri-e-yo.]

A: 아, 오늘 수요일 아니었어요?
[a, o-neul su-yo-il a-ni-eo-sseo-yo?]

B: 네. 오늘 화요일이에요.
[ne. o-neul hwa-yo-i-ri-e-yo.]

A: What day is it today?

B: It is Tuesday.

A: Oh, wasn't today Wednesday?

B: No, today is Tuesday.

36

✏ Exercises for Lesson 5

Match the Korean words to the English equivalent.

1. 일요일   a. Saturday

2. 화요일   b. Sunday

3. 토요일   c. Thursday

4. 목요일   d. Monday

5. 수요일   e. Friday

6. 월요일   f. Wednesday

7. 금요일   g. Tuesday

Check the answers on **p.196**

37

Telling Time, and More

LESSON 6

But, However

그렇지만, 그런데

Jump right back into Korean conjunctions with this lesson, since now we will introduce two more words that can be used at the beginning of sentences!

그렇지만 = but, however

그런데 = but, however

(1) 피곤해요. 그렇지만 영화 보고 싶어요.
[pi-gon-hae-yo. geu-reo-chi-man yeong-hwa bo-go si-peo-yo.]
= I am tired, but I want to see a movie.

(2) 피곤해요. 그런데 영화 보고 싶어요.
[pi-gon-hae-yo. geu-reon-de yeong-hwa bo-go si-peo-yo.]
= I am tired. However, I want to see a movie.

38

그렇지만 and 그런데 both mean "but" or "however", but there is some difference in the usage of these two words.

(1) 어제 이거 샀어요. 그렇지만 정말 커요.
[eo-je i-geo sa-sseo-yo. geu-reo-chi-man jeong-mal keo-yo.]
= I bought this yesterday. "그렇지만" it is really big.

(2) 어제 이거 샀어요. 그런데 정말 커요.
[eo-je i-geo sa-sseo-yo. geu-reon-de jeong-mal keo-yo.]
= I bought this yesterday. "그런데" it is really big.

In sentence (1), 그렇지만 means "but" or "however". The speaker is contrasting two facts: having purchased "this" yesterday and "it" being too big. It sounds as if the speaker is disappointed that it is very big.

Track 11

In sentence (2), the intended meaning is "but", however at the same time it can also mean "and". If the speaker is implying the meaning of "and", the entire sentence can mean "I bought this yesterday, and as I have come to find out, it is really big".

In summary,
그렇지만 = "but"
그런데 = "but" or "and" (depending on the context)

To contrast two sentences, "A + however/but + B", you can choose to use either 그렇지만 or 그런데.

To introduce two actions or states which occurred one after another, and if the first sentence is background information for the second, only use 그런데.

어제 학교에 갔어요. 그렇지만 일요일이었어요.
[eo-je hak-kkyo-e ga-sseo-yo. geu-reo-chi-man i-ryo-i-ri-eo-sseo-yo.]
= I went to school yesterday, but it was Sunday.

어제 학교에 갔어요. 그런데 일요일이었어요.
[eo-je hak-kkyo-e ga-sseo-yo. geu-reon-de i-ryo-i-ri-eo-sseo-yo.]
= I went to school yesterday, but it was Sunday.

= I went to school yesterday, and by the way, it was Sunday.

= I went to school yesterday, and as I found out after I went, it was Sunday.

그런데 can be used for a wider variety of meanings than 그렇지만, which has a very formal nuance to it and is used more in writing. In actual everyday conversations, 그런데 is used more often than 그렇지만.

Sample Sentences

Track 11

어젯밤 늦게 잤어요. 그런데 피곤하지 않아요.
[eo-jet-ppam neut-kke ja-sseo-yo. geu-reon-de pi-gon-ha-ji a-na-yo.]
= I went to bed late last night, but I am not tired.

늦게 = late, at a late hour

피곤하다 = to be tired

저는 매일 운동을 해요. 그런데 살이 빠지지 않아요.
[jeo-neun mae-il un-dong-eul hae-yo. geu-reon-de sa-ri ppa-ji-ji a-na-yo.]
= I work out every day, but I do not lose any weight.

매일 = every day

살이 빠지다 = to lose weight

저는 친구가 없어요. 그런데 왕따는 아니에요.
[jeo-neun chin-gu-ga eop-sseo-yo. geu-reon-de wang-tta-neun a-ni-e-yo.]
= I do not have friends, but I am not a loner.

왕따 = outcast, loner, someone who is bullied by others

Sample Dialogue

Track 12

A: 저 어젯밤에 일찍 잤어요.
[jeo eo-jet-ppa-me il-jjik ja-sseo-yo.]

B: 윤아 씨가요?
[yu-na ssi-ga-yo?]

A: 네. 그런데 오늘 아침에 늦게 일어났어요.
[ne. geu-reon-de o-neul a-chi-me neut-kke i-reo-na-sseo-yo.]

A: I went to bed early last night.

B: Who? You?

A: Yes, but I got up late this morning.

✏ *Exercises for Lesson* **6**

Check the answers on **p.196**

Translate the following words or phrases to Korean:

1. "But" or "however"

(   )

2. "I am tired, but I want to see a movie."

(   )

3. "It is good, but it is expensive."

(   )

4. "Yesterday, it rained, but now, it does not rain."

(   )

5. "I went to school yesterday, but it was Sunday."

(   )

Conjunctions, Tenses,

LESSON 7

"To" someone, "From" someone

-한테, -한테서

Track 13

When it comes to particles in Korean, there are not always direct (or correct) translations from Korean to English. It is important to understand the roles the particles play within the sentence rather than just trying to memorize a similar English counterpart.

Keep that in mind as you learn about the particles -한테 and -한테서!
[-han-te]   [-han-te-seo]

In order to express "to" or "from" someone in Korean, the particles -한테 and -한테서 are used most commonly. There are two other particles which have similar characteristics (-에게 and -에게서) but are used mainly in written language and will not be covered in this lesson.
[-e-ge]
[-e-ge-seo]

-한테 = "to" someone, "from" someone

-한테서 = "from" someone

-한테 can mean both "to" and "from" someone, whereas -한테서 can only mean "from" someone. The meaning of -한테 can only be completely understood by examining the context of a sentence.

-한테 and -한테서 can ONLY be used about people or animals, NOT objects or places.

- "to a friend" = friend + -한테 (O)
- "to Seoul" = Seoul + -한테 (X)

Ex)

저한테 = to me, from me
[jeo-han-te]
친구한테 = to a friend, from a friend
[chin-gu-han-te]
누구한테 = to whom, from whom
[nu-gu-han-te]

저한테서 = from me
[jeo-han-te-seo]
친구한테서 = from a friend
[chin-gu-han-te-seo]
누구한테서 = from whom
[nu-gu-han-te-seo]

Track 13

* *When used with a verb that already expresses passive voice, -한테 can also mean "by".*
For example, 맞다 generally means "to be correct", but in another sentence, it can mean "to be beaten" or "to be hit". Therefore, A한테 맞다 can be translated to English as "to be beaten by A".
[mat-tta]

Conjunctions, Tenses,

Sample Dialogue

Track
14

A: 저한테 이메일 보냈어요?
[jeo-han-te i-me-il bo-nae-sseo-yo?]

B: 네.
[ne.]

A: 언제 보냈어요?
[eon-je bo-nae-sseo-yo?]

B: 왜요? 안 왔어요?
[wae-yo? an wa-sseo-yo?]

A: Did you email me?

B: Yes.

A: When did you send it?

B: Why? It hasn't arrived?

Telling Time, and More

✏ Exercises for Lesson 7

Check the answers on **p.196**

1. 받다 means "to receive" in English. How do you say "I received it from a friend" in Korean?
[bat-tta]

(   )

2. If 물어보다 is "to ask", how would you write "(to) Whom did you ask?"
[mu-reo-bo-da]

(   )

3. 질문 is "question". How do you say "Do you have a question for me?"
[jil-mun]

(   )

4. Since 동생 is "younger brother/sister" and 주다 is "to give", how do you say "I will give this to
[dong-saeng] [ju-da]
my younger brother/sister"?

(   )

5. 얻다 is "to obtain; to acquire; to get". How do you write "I got this from my friend"?
[eot-tta]

(   )

46

LESSON **8**

Telling Time

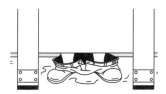

한 시, 두 시, 세 시, 네 시 …

Now it is TIME to talk about **TIME**!

Track 15

As you may have already studied (if you studied with the Level 1 book in this series, you have definitely already studied this!), there are two number systems in Korean. Most of the time, the two number systems are used for different things or they are interchangeable. When it comes to telling time, however, both systems are used at the same time.

Quickly review some **native Korean numbers**:

1 하나 [ha-na]	5 다섯 [da-seot]	9 아홉 [a-hop]
2 둘 [dul]	6 여섯 [yeo-seot]	10 열 [yeol]
3 셋 [set]	7 일곱 [il-gop]	11 열하나 [yeo-ra-na]
4 넷 [net]	8 여덟 [yeo-deol]	12 열둘 [yeol-ttul]

When saying the hour, use these native Korean numbers (1, 2, 3 and 4 are irregular and change form a little).

Conjugation

Number + 시 = hour

하나 + 시 = 한 시 = 1 o'clock (not 하나 시)
[han si]
둘 + 시 = 두 시 = 2 o'clock (not 둘 시)
[du si]
셋 + 시 = 세 시 = 3 o'clock (not 셋 시)
[se si]
넷 + 시 = 네 시 = 4 o'clock (not 넷 시)
[ne si]
다섯 시 = 5 o'clock
[da-seot si]
여섯 시 = 6 o'clock
[yeo-seot si]
일곱 시 = 7 o'clock
[il-gop si]
여덟 시 = 8 o'clock
[yeo-deol si]
아홉 시 = 9 o'clock
[a-hop si]
열 시 = 10 o'clock
[yeol si]
열한 시 = 11 o'clock
[yeo-ran si]
열두 시 = 12 o'clock
[yeol-ttu si]

Track 15

Now, take a minute to review some **sino-Korean numbers**:

1 일	2 이	3 삼	4 사	5 오
[il]	[i]	[sam]	[sa]	[o]
6 육	7 칠	8 팔	9 구	10 십
[yuk]	[chil]	[pal]	[gu]	[sip]

* Numbers 11 and onward are combinations of these 10 numbers.

When saying minutes in Korean, use sino-Korean numbers.

Conjugation

Number + 분 = minute
[bun]

일 분 = 1 minute

이 분 = 2 minutes

오 분 = 5 minutes

십 분 = 10 minutes

십오 분 = 15 minutes
[si-bo bun]

삼십 분 = 30 minutes
[sam-sip bun]

오십오 분 = 55 minutes
[o-si-bo bun]

Track 15

1:05 = 1 + 시 + 5 + 분 = 한 시 오 분

1:15 = 1 + 시 + 15 + 분 = 한 시 십오 분

3:20 = 3 + 시 + 20 + 분 = 세 시 이십 분
[i-sip bun]

10:00 = 10 + 시 = 열 시

10:30 = 10 + 시 + 30 + 분 = 열 시 삼십 분

* *"# o'clock sharp" is expressed with the word* 정각*.*
[jeong-gak]
** *Rather than saying* 삼십 분*, the word* 반*, meaning "half", can also be used.*
[ban]

49

Telling Time, and More

How to ask the time

지금 몇 시예요?
[ji-geum myeot si-ye-yo?]
= What time is it now?

지금 몇 시 몇 분이에요?
[ji-geum myeot si myeot bu-ni-e-yo?]
= What is the hour, and what is the minute?

Sample Sentences

🎙
**Track
15**

저는 매일 아침 9시까지 출근해요.
[jeo-neun mae-il a-chim a-hop-si-kka-ji chul-geun-hae-yo.]
= I get to work by 9 o'clock every morning.

매일 = every day

출근하다 = to go/get to work
[chul-geun-ha-da]

내일 수업이 4시 반에 끝나요.
[nae-il su-eo-bi ne-si ba-ne kkeun-na-yo.]
= My classes finish at 4:30 tomorrow.

내일 = tomorrow

수업 = class
[su-eop]
끝나다 = to finish
[kkeun-na-da]

오늘 몇 시에 친구를 만나요?
[o-neul myeot si-e chin-gu-reul man-na-yo?]
= What time do you meet your friend today?

만나다 = to meet
[man-na-da]

50

Sample Dialogue

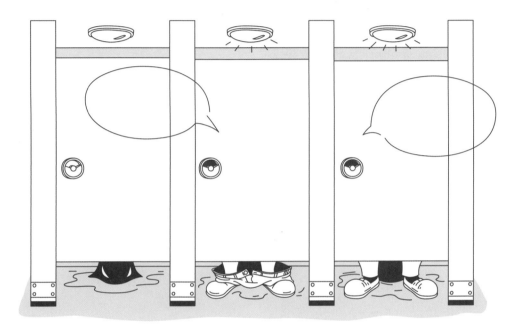

Track 16

A: 오늘 몇 시에 출근했어요?
[o-neul myeot si-e chul-geun-hae-sseo-yo?]

B: 아홉 시 반에 출근했어요. 유정 씨는요?
[a-hop si ba-ne chul-geun-hae-sseo-yo. yu-jeong ssi-neun-nyo?]

A: 여덟 시 십 분에 출근했어요.
[yeo-deol si sip bu-ne chul-geun-hae-sseo-yo.]

A: *What time did you come to work today?*

B: *I came to work at 9:30. How about you, Yujeong?*

A: *I came to work at 8:10.*

✎ Exercises for Lesson 8

1. How do you say "What time is it?" in Korean?

( )

2. Please write out "*3* o'clock" using only 한글.

( )

3. In Korean, how do you say "*1:15*" (time)?

( )

4. Please write out "*5:47*" using only 한글.

( )

5. How is "*10:30*" (time) read in Korean?

( )

Conjunctions, Tenses,

LESSON **9**

Counters

개, 명

When counting in English, the number is followed by the word for what is being counted (i.e. a person, two cats, three houses). In Korean, there are many words used as counting units for different subjects which are similar to words in English such as "loaf" of bread, "glass" of water, "sticks" of butter, and "cubes" of ice.

Track 17

There are SO many counters in Korean that it is impossible to memorize them all at once. Learning the counters one by one as you practice or as you need them is a little less overwhelming and may help you learn them more efficiently.

Ex)

English: number + noun	**Korean: noun + number + counter**
1. a car	1. "car" + one + "counter for cars"
2. two pencils	2. "pencil" + two + "counter for pencils"
3. three books	3. "book" + three + "counter for books"

53

There are literally hundreds of counters in the Korean language, but not all of them are always used. As long as the speakers understand each other, some people just use the simplest and easiest counter to count certain words and it does not confuse anyone. For example, in Korean, a pencil is 연필 and the counter for pencils is 자루. The word 자루 is also
[yeon-pil]   [ja-ru]
used for counting pens, bags containing grain, and knives. Instead of using the word 자루 all the time for 연필, many people just use the general counter for things, which is 개.
[gae]

연필 한 자루 = one pencil
[yeon-pil han ja-ru]
연필 한 개 = one pencil
[yeon-pil han gae]

Track 17

This does NOT work for all counters. Some common counters are almost never replaced with 개. For example, the counter for cars is 대, and it is never replaced with 개. In other
[dae]
words, changing 연필 한 자루 to 연필 한 개 is okay, but changing 차 한 대 to 차 한 개 is not okay and considered incorrect.

The counter 대 is used more frequently than the counter 자루. However, as a learner of the Korean language, if you find yourself using the wrong counter, you will be given feedback so you will remember better next time. It is better to say something in Korean than choosing not to say anything at all! Making mistakes is part of the learning process, so do not be too hard on yourself when you mess up. The person listening to you will, more than likely, be impressed with your skills anyway and just offer the correction without judgment.

In this lesson, remember these two most frequently used counters, 개 and 명.
[myeong]

개 as a noun in Korean means "dog", but when used as a counter, it is used for counting things and objects. 명 is used for counting people.

The majority of the time, counters are used with native Korean numbers.

Conjugation

Numbers + 개 (counter for things)

1 = 하나 → 한 개
[ha-na]   [han]

2 = 둘 → 두 개
[dul]   [du]

3 = 셋 → 세 개
[set]   [se]

4 = 넷 → 네 개
[net]   [ne]

5 = 다섯 → 다섯 개
[da-seot]

6 = 여섯 → 여섯 개
[yeo-seot]

7 = 일곱 → 일곱 개
[il-gop]

8 = 여덟 → 여덟 개
[yeo-deol]

9 = 아홉 → 아홉 개
[a-hop]

10 = 열 → 열 개
[yeol]

> *Do you remember the irregularity rule
> for these numbers (plus 20)?*

**Track
17**

From 11 to 20

열한 개, 열두 개, 열세 개, 열네 개, 열다섯 개, 열여섯 개, 열일곱 개, 열여덟 개,
[yeol-han] [yeol-ttu] [yeol-sse] [yeol-le] [yeol-tta-seot] [yeol-lyeo-seot] [yeol-lil-gop] [yeol-lyeo-deol]

열아홉 개, 스무 개
[yeo-ra-hop] [seu-mu]

From 21 to 30

스물한 개, 스물두 개, 스물세 개, 스물네 개, 스물다섯 개, 스물여섯 개, 스물일곱 개,
[seu-mul-han] [seu-mul-ttu] [seu-mul-sse] [seu-mul-le] [seu-mul-da-seot] [seu-mul-lyeo-seot] [seu-mu-ril-gop]

스물여덟 개, 스물아홉 개, 서른 개
[seu-mul-lyeo-deol] [seu-mu-ra-hop] [seo-reun]

55

Ex)

one apple = 사과 + 1 + 개 = 사과 한 개
[sa-gwa]

two stones = 돌 + 2 + 개 = 돌 두 개
[dol]

five balls = 공 + 5 + 개 = 공 다섯 개
[gong]

how many (things) = 몇 + 개 = 몇 개
[myeot]

Use the counter 명 for "people".

one person = 한 명

two students = 학생 + 2 + 명 = 학생 두 명
[hak-ssaeng]

three friends = 친구 + 3 + 명 = 친구 세 명
[chin-gu]

how many (people) = 몇 + 명 = 몇 명

Track 17

The word for "people" or "person", 사람, is also used when generally referring to a small
[sa-ram]
number of people without specifying who they are.

Ex)

Q: How many people are there?

A: There are 10 people.

= Q: 몇 명 있어요?
[myeot myeong i-sseo-yo?]
A: 10명 있어요.
[yeol myeong i-sseo-yo.]

= Q: 몇 사람 있어요?

A: 열 사람 있어요. (This is unnatural).

→ A: 두 사람 있어요. (two people - this is okay).

Check out a few more commonly used counters:

병 = bottles
[byeong]

　　몇 병 = how many bottles
　　[myeot byeong]

마리 = animals
[ma-ri]

　　개 한 마리 = one dog
　　[gae han ma-ri]

　　새 한 마리 = one bird
　　[sae han ma-ri]

　　오리 세 마리 = three ducks
　　[o-ri se ma-ri]

대 = vehicles, machinery
[dae]

　　차 한 대 = one car
　　[cha han dae]

　　비행기 세 대 = three airplanes
　　[bi-haeng-gi se dae]

권 = books
[gwon]

　　책 한 권 = one book
　　[chaek han gwon]

　　책 두 권 = two books
　　[chaek du gwon]

장 = paper, pages, tickets
[jang]

　　종이 한 장 = a sheet of paper
　　[jong-i han jang]

Track 17

Sample Sentences

아줌마 김치찌개 한 개 주세요.
[a-jum-ma gim-chi-jji-gae han gae ju-se-yo.]
= Ma'am, please give me one kimchi stew.

　　찌개 = stew

콜라 한 병 주세요.
[kol-la han byeong ju-se-yo.]
= Please give me a bottle of cola.

Sample Dialogue

Track 18

A: 의자 몇 개 필요해요?
[ui-ja myeot gae pi-ryo-hae-yo?]

B: 스무 개요.
[seu-mu gae-yo.]

A: 지금 스무 명 있어요?
[ji-geum seu-mu myeong i-sseo-yo?]

B: 아니요. 그런데 곧 올 거예요.
[a-ni-yo. geu-reon-de got ol kkeo-ye-yo.]

A: How many chairs do you need?

B: 20 chairs.

A: Are there 20 people now?

B: No, but people will come soon.

Conjunctions, Tenses,

✎ Exercises for Lesson 9

Translate the following to Korean.

1. When counting objects: "three things".

( )

2. When counting people: "five people".

( )

3. How do you write "three chairs" in Korean? The word for "chair" is 의자.
[ui-ja]

( )

4. "How many people are there?"

( )

5. "There are two people."

( )

Check the answers on **p.197**

LESSON 10

Present Progressive

-고 있어요

Track 19

Don't be "tense" about another lesson on tenses! You will be able to form sentences in the present progressive tense (현재 진행형) in Korean.
[hyeon-jae jin-haeng-hyeong]

Examples of present progressive sentences in English:

1. I am reading a book.

2. What are you watching?

3. He is helping me a lot.

> ## Conjugation
>
> - to be -ing = Verb stem + **-고 있다**
> [-go it-tta]
>
> **보다** = to see
> [bo-da]
>
> **보고 있다** = to be seeing
> [bo-go it-tta]

Conjunctions, Tenses,

Present progressive:

- am/are/is -ing = Verb stem + **-고 있어요**
[-go i-sseo-yo]

밖에 비가 오고 있어요. = It is raining outside.
[ba-kke bi-ga o-go i-sseo-yo.]
밖에 눈이 오고 있어요. = It is snowing outside.
[ba-kke nu-ni o-go i-sseo-yo.]
밖에 바람이 불고 있어요. = The wind is blowing outside.
[ba-kke ba-ra-mi bul-go i-sseo-yo.]

Past progressive:

- was/were -ing = Verb stem + **-고 있었어요**
[-go i-sseo-sseo-yo]

눈이 오고 있었어요. = It was snowing.
[nu-ni o-go i-sseo-sseo-yo.]
비가 오고 있었어요. = It was raining.
[bi-ga o-go i-sseo-sseo-yo.]
바람이 불고 있었어요. = The wind was blowing.
[ba-ra-mi bul-go i-sseo-sseo-yo.]
경은 씨가 자고 있었어요. = Kyeong-eun was sleeping.
[gyeong-eun ssi-ga ja-go i-sseo-sseo-yo.]

Track
19

Future progressive:

- will be -ing = Verb stem + **-고 있을 거예요**
[-go i-sseul kkeo-ye-yo]

Past and future progressive sentences are quite common in Korean and are used almost every day. Having a thorough understanding of how to use the present progressive form will make learning past and future progressive quite easy.

When using the present progressive tense, there are two important points to remember:

1

Literal translation between Korean present progressive sentences and English present progressive sentences does not always work, especially when using the present progressive form in English to indicate the future.

For example, "I am not going to work tomorrow" in English is talking about the future; therefore in Korean, -고 있어요 cannot be used.

2

Track 19

In everyday conversations, sentences which need to be in the present progressive form do not always take the -고 있어요 form. Koreans often just use the plain present tense form even for sentences that would normally be present progressive tense in English.

Ex)

Instead of saying:

A: 지금 뭐 하고 있어요? = What are you doing now?
[ji-geum mwo ha-go i-sseo-yo?]
   B: 공부하고 있어요. = I am studying.
[gong-bu-ha-go i-sseo-yo.]

many people say:

A: 지금 뭐 해요? = What are you doing now?
[ji-geum mwo hae-yo?]
   B: 공부해요. = I am studying.
[gong-bu-hae-yo.]

Sample Sentences

일하다 = to work
[i-ra-da]
일하고 있어요. = I am working.
[i-ra-go i-sseo-yo.]
일하고 있었어요. = I was working.

일하고 있을 거예요. = I will be working.

듣다 = to listen
[deut-tta]
듣고 있어요. = I am listening.
[deut-kko i-sseo-yo.]
듣고 있었어요. = I was listening.

듣고 있을 거예요. = I will be listening.

생각하다 = to think
[saeng-ga-ka-da]
생각하고 있어요. = I am thinking.
[saeng-ga-ka-go i-sseo-yo.]
생각하고 있었어요. = I was thinking.

생각하고 있을 거예요. = I will be thinking.

Track 19

졸다 = to doze off
[jol-da]
졸고 있어요. = I am dozing off.
[jol-go i-sseo-yo.]
졸고 있었어요. = I was dozing off.

졸고 있을 거예요. = I will be dozing off.

Sample Dialogue

A: 그 영상 봤어요?
[geu yeong-sang bwa-sseo-yo?]

B: 지금 보고 있어요.
[ji-geum bo-go i-sseo-yo.]

A: 재미있어요?
[jae-mi-i-sseo-yo?]

B: 네, 재미있어요.
[ne, jae-mi-i-sseo-yo.]

A: Have you watched the video?

B: I am watching it now.

A: Is it interesting?

B: Yes, it is interesting.

✏ *Exercises for Lesson* **10**

Check the answers on **p.197**

Translate the following sentences to Korean:

I. "I am reading a book."

(읽다 = to read)
[ik-tta]

(   )

2. "What are you doing?"

(   )

3. "What were you doing?"

(   )

4. "I was sleeping."

(   )

5. "I will be studying."

(   )

NAMSAN
(남산)

남산 (Namsan, literally "South Mountain") stands in the middle of Seoul, surrounded by major shopping districts and an ever-growing and modernizing city. However, many generations ago, 남산 marked the southern border of Seoul.

This mountain is easily accessible from many different points in Seoul because of its central location. For example, it is a 20-30 minute walk from Subway lines 1 or 2, 시청역 (City Hall Station) in Jung-gu. It is also right outside of Subway line 6, 한강진역 (Hangangjin Station) and very close to Subway line 3, 동대입구역 (Dongguk University Station).

There is more to 남산 than N. Seoul Tower, a.k.a. Namsan Tower or 남산타워. One of the most popular destinations aside from the tower for tourists and Seoulites alike during the springtime is the Namsan Circular Road that connects the Namsan Library to the Palgakjeong. The cherry blossom trees that line this road are absolutely beautiful and well worth the hike to get there.

Almost every part of 남산 is full of lush, natural green landscape that offers a great contrast to the tall buildings and paved streets of the surrounding metropolis. The entire mountain and surrounding area is known as 남산 공원 (Namsan Park). 남산 공원 contains many places of interest, including the National Theater, Namsan Public Library, and several statues in memorial of Korean patriots. The park also contains Palgakjeong (an octagonal pavilion), an aquarium, a fountain, and a cable car leading to Seoul Tower.

Since 남산 is, well, a 산, an added benefit of the placement of this mountain is that you can enjoy hiking without having to travel very far away. While hiking one of the many trails on 남산, you can enjoy the multitude of trees, plants, and animals as well as take advantage of the exercise equipment. You might have to fight off some 아줌마 or 아저씨 to use it, but it'll be a good way to practice your Korean!

남산 is also one of the best places in Seoul to get a panoramic view of the city. Whether you go during the day or at night, you won't be disappointed. There are various photo spots and viewing platforms along the walking trails that give you the best view possible and help you catch spectacular photos of your memories that will last a lifetime.

Congratulations!
You've made it past lesson 10!
You're nearly half way finished with Level 2!
화이팅!

LESSON 11

Self Introduction

자기소개

Track 21

By using what you have learned so far, you can already express many things about yourself. In this lesson, you will add to that knowledge and learn vocabulary, phrases, and sentence patterns which are specific and absolutely necessary for introducing yourself in Korean.

자기소개 self-introduction
[ja-gi-so-gae]

There are thousands of different things you could reveal when introducing yourself, but to generalize, some of the most common information is:

- name

- age

- place of living

- work

Conjunctions, Tenses,

- school

- family members

- hobby

- greetings

Self-introductions are personal, and each situation is different. You may feel like revealing a lot of information about yourself, or just a little, so there is no need to try to memorize every sentence related to introductions. No single detailed chapter on self-introductions can cover everything you need to know every time you introduce yourself.

There are a few frequently used sentence patterns to use whenever you introduce yourself.

I. ABC은/는 XYZ이에요. = ABC is XYZ.
[ABC-eun/neun XYZ-i-e-yo.]

Track 21

Ex)

I am a student. = 저는 학생이에요.
[jeo-neun hak-ssaeng-i-e-yo.]

I am a teacher. = 저는 선생님이에요.
[jeo-neun seon-saeng-ni-mi-e-yo.]

I am James. = 저는 제임스예요.
[jeo-neun je-im-sseu-ye-yo.]

My name is Stephen. = 제 이름은 스티븐이에요.
[je i-reu-meun seu-ti-beu-ni-e-yo.]

My sister's name is Taliana. = 제 여동생 이름은 탈리아나예요.
[je yeo-dong-saeng i-reu-meun tal-li-a-na-ye-yo.]

I am 30 years old. = 저는 30살이에요.
[jeo-neun seo-reun-sa-ri-e-yo.]

My name is Choi Kyeungeun. = 제 이름은 최경은이에요.
[je i-reu-meun choe-gyeong-eu-ni-e-yo.]

My age is a secret. = 제 나이는 비밀이에요.
[je na-i-neun bi-mi-ri-e-yo.]

And I am a Korean teacher. = 그리고 저는 한국어 선생님이에요.
[geu-ri-go jeo-neun han-gu-geo seon-saeng-ni-mi-e-yo.]

71

2. ABC은/는 XYZ이/가 + VERB = As for ABC, XYZ + VERB.
[ABC-eun/neun XYZ-i/ga]

Ex)

저는 여동생이 있어요. = I have a younger sister. (lit. "As for me, a younger sister exists".)
[jeo-neun yeo-dong-saeng-i i-sseo-yo.]
저는 남동생이 있어요. = I have a younger brother.
[jeo-neun nam-dong-saeng-i i-sseo-yo.]
저는 언니가 있어요. = I have an older sister.
[jeo-neun eon-ni-ga i-sseo-yo.]
저는 취미가 없어요. = I do not have any hobbies. (lit. "As for me, the hobby does not exist".)
[jeo-neun chwi-mi-ga eop-sseo-yo.]
저는 취미가 수영이에요. = My hobby is swimming. (lit. "As for me, the hobby, swimming is".)
[jeo-neun chwi-mi-ga su-yeong-i-e-yo.]

3. ABC은/는 XYZ에/에서 + VERB = ABC + VERB + in XYZ.
[ABC-eun/neun XYZ-e/e-seo]

Ex)

저는 서울에 살아요. = I live in Seoul.
[jeo-neun seo-u-re sa-ra-yo.]
저는 은행에서 일해요. = I work in a bank.
[jeo-neun eun-haeng-e-seo il-hae-yo.]
저는 대학교에서 중국어를 가르쳐요. = I teach Chinese in college.
[jeo-neun dae-hak-kkyo-e-seo jung-gu-geo-reul ga-reu-chyeo-yo.]
저는 미국에서 태어났어요. = I was born in the USA.
[jeo-neun mi-gu-ge-seo tae-eo-na-sseo-yo.]

Important and useful vocabulary words:

나이 = age
[na-i]
취미 = hobby
[chwi-mi]
직장 = workplace
[jik-jjang]
직업 = job = 하는 일
[ji-geop]   [ha-neun il]
사는 곳 = place of living
[sa-neun got]
가족 = family
[ga-jok]

Conjunctions, Tenses,

친척 = relatives, extended family
[chin-cheok]
대학생 = university student
[dae-hak-ssaeng]
고등학생 = high school student
[go-deung-hak-ssaeng]
중학생 = middle school student
[jung-hak-ssaeng]
초등학생 = elementary school student
[cho-deung-hak-ssaeng]

Useful greetings:

처음 뵙겠습니다. = How do you do?
[cheo-eum boep-kket-sseum-ni-da.]
반갑습니다. = It is nice to meet you.
[ban-gap-sseum-ni-da.]
제 명함이에요. = It is my business card.
[je myeong-ha-mi-e-yo.]
다음에 또 뵐게요. = See you again next time.
[da-eu-me tto boel-kke-yo.]
이야기 많이 들었어요. = I have heard a lot about you.
[i-ya-gi ma-ni deu-reo-sseo-yo.]

**Track
21**

Telling Time, and More

Sample Dialogue

Track 22

A: 안녕하세요. 처음 뵙겠습니다.
[an-nyeong-ha-se-yo. cheo-eum boep-kket-sseum-ni-da.]

B: 안녕하세요.
[an-nyeong-ha-se-yo.]

A: 저는 지금 대학교에서 한국어를
공부하고 있어요.
[jeo-neun ji-geum dae-hak-kkyo-e-seo han-gu-geo-reul
gong-bu-ha-go i-sseo-yo.]

B: 아! 반갑습니다. 저는 온라인에서
한국어를 가르치고 있어요.
[a! ban-gap-sseum-ni-da. jeo-neun ol-la-i-ne-seo
han-gu-geo-reul ga-reu-chi-go i-sseo-yo.]

A: Hello. How do you do?

B: Hello.

A: I am currently studying the Korean
language at university.

B: Oh! Nice to meet you. I am teaching
the Korean language online.

✏ Exercises for Lesson 11

Translate the following phrases to Korean:

1. "I am a student."

( )

2. "My name is Minsu."
  (이름 = name, 제 이름 = "My name")

( )

3. "I am *20* years old."

( )

Check the answers on **p.197**

4. "I live in Seoul."

( )

5. "It is nice to meet you."

( )

LESSON 12

What is the Date?

마이클 씨는 방학이 언제예요?

AM 11:11

마이클 ♥   AM 11:13

7월부터 8월까지요.

날짜

Track
23

After studying with this lesson, you will be able to say and identify the months of the year and the days in a month in Korean. You will also be able to answer questions regarding the date as well as ask questions related to dates.

Names of the months

In Korean, the names for the 12 months in a year are very simple. Just add the word 월,
[wol]
which means "month", after every corresponding sino-Korean number.

January = 1월
[i-rwol]

February = 2월
[i-wol]

March = 3월
[sa-mwol]

April = 4월
[sa-wol]

May = 5월
[o-wol]

June = 6월
[yu-wol]

July = 7월
[chi-rwol]

August = 8월
[pa-rwol]

September = 9월
[gu-wol]

October = 10월
[si-wol]

November = 11월
[si-bi-rwol]

December = 12월
[si-bi-wol]

Which month: 몇 월
[myeot wol = myeo-dwol]

Conjunctions, Tenses,

Days in a month

Simply add the sino-Korean number to the Korean word 일, which means "day".
[il]

Ex)

1 + 일 = 1일
[i-ril]
2 + 일 = 2일
[i-il]
⋮
29 + 일 = 29일
[i-sip-kku-il]
30 + 일 = 30일
[sam-si-bil]

What date: 며칠
[myeo-chil]

* *The expression 몇 월 is a simple combination of 몇(which, how many) and 월(month), whereas 며칠 doesn't use 일 as a component. It's often misunderstood as a mix of 몇 and 일(day), so you will see a lot of Korean speakers writing it as 몇 일, too.*

What month and what date: 몇 월 며칠
[myeo-dwol myeo-chil]

Sample Sentences

몇 월 며칠이에요? = What is the date?
[myeo-dwol myeo-chi-ri-e-yo?]
오늘 몇 월 며칠이에요? = What is today's date?
[o-neul]
생일이 몇 월 며칠이에요? = What date is your birthday?
[saeng-i-ri]

When mentioning a specific day, 언제, which means "when", can also be used.
[eon-je]
생일이 언제예요? = When is your birthday?
[eon-je-ye-yo?]

77

Telling Time, and More

Sample Dialogue

Track 24

A: 마이클 씨는 방학이 언제예요?
[ma-i-keul ssi-neun bang-ha-gi eon-je-ye-yo?]

B: 7월부터 8월까지요.
[chi-rwol-bu-teo pa-rwol-kka-ji-yo.]

A: 7월 1일부터요?
[chi-rwol i-ril-bu-teo-yo?]

B: 아니요. 7월 5일부터요.
[a-ni-yo. chi-rwol o-il-bu-teo-yo.]

A: When is your school vacation, Michael?

B: It is from July to August.

A: Starting July 1st?

B: No. It starts July 5th.

✎ Exercises for Lesson 12

1. In Korean, the word for month is 월. How do you say September?

( )

2. What is the word for "day" or "days" in Korean?

( )

3. How do you say "September 25th"?

( )

4. How do you ask "What month?"

( )

5. How do you ask "What date?"

( )

6. How do you ask "What date is your birthday?"

( )

Check the answers on **p.197**

LESSON **13**

Too, Also

-도 (Part I)

Track 25

If you have been studying with this book series starting with Level I, you have learned a handful of different particles up to this point: -이/가 (subject marking particles), -은/는 (topic [-i/ga] [-eun/neun] marking particles), and -을/를 (object marking particles). Are you ready to add one more [-eul/reul] particle to the bunch? :D

-도 is used to represent the meaning of **"also"** and **"too"**.
[-do]

In English, the placement of the words "too", "also", or "as well" varies depending on the speaker. Most of the time they are added to the end of a sentence, but sometimes they can be placed in the middle or near the beginning next to the subject. In Korean, however, -도 is treated as a particle and ALWAYS follows the noun or pronoun.

Ex)

I. I like it, too.

저도 좋아요.
[jeo-do jo-a-yo.]

2. I think so as well.

   저도 그런 것 같아요.
   [jeo-do geu-reon geot ga-ta-yo.]
3. I, too, saw it.

   저도 봤어요.
   [jeo-do bwa-sseo-yo.]

In these sentences "too" and "as well" were used to modify different things. In the last sentence, "I, too, saw it", the word "too" is modifying "I". If you literally translate this to Korean, it becomes "저도 봤어요". Adding -도 right after 저, which means "I", in this case
   [jeo-do bwa-sseo-yo.]
modifies "I" just as in the English sentence.

When the particle -도 needs to be attached to a noun or a pronoun which already has a particle behind it, -도 can replace the particle.

Track 25

Sample Sentences

I am a student.

= 저는 학생이에요.
   [jeo-neun hak-ssaeng-i-e-yo.]
I am a student, too.

= 저도 학생이에요.
   [jeo-do hak-ssaeng-i-e-yo.]
 * Note that it is NOT "저는도 학생이에요".

I brought this.

= 이것 가져왔어요.
   [i-geot ga-jeo-wa-sseo-yo.]
I brought this, too.

= 이것도 가져왔어요.
   [i-geot-tto ga-jeo-wa-sseo-yo.]

Do you work today?

= 오늘 일해요?
[o-neul il-hae-yo?]

Do you work today as well?

= 오늘도 일해요?
[o-neul-do il-hae-yo?]

Depending on the location of the particle -도, the meaning of the entire sentence can change.

In Korean, "please give me water" is said as "물 주세요".
[mul ju-se-yo]

To say "give water to me, too, not just other people", say: 저도 물 주세요.
[jeo-do]

Track 25

"Please give some water to me, too". = 저도 물 주세요.

To say "give me, not only other things, but water as well", say: 저 물도 주세요.
[jeo mul-do ju-se-yo.]

"Please also give some water to me". = 저 물도 주세요.

Sample Dialogue

Track 26

A: 오늘도 야근해요?
[o-neul-do ya-geun-hae-yo?]

B: 네. 알렉스 씨도 야근하고 있어요?
[ne. al-lek-sseu ssi-do ya-geun-ha-go i-sseo-yo?]

A: 네.
[ne.]

B: 힘내세요. 파이팅!
[him-nae-se-yo. pa-i-ting!]

A: *Do you work overtime today as well?*

B: *Yes. Are you also working overtime, Alex?*

A: *Yes.*

B: *Cheer up. Let's do this!*

✏ Exercises for Lesson 13

Check the answers on **p.197**

1. "I am a teacher" is "저는 선생님이에요."
[jeo-neun seon-saeng-ni-mi-e-yo.]
Please write "I am a teacher, too" in Korean.

( )

2. "Do you study Korean?" is "한국어 공부해요?"
[han-gu-geo gong-bu-hae-yo?]
How do you ask "Do you study Korean, too (in addition to other languages)?"

( )

3. "Do you work today?" is "오늘 일해요?"
[o-neul il-hae-yo?]
How do you ask "Do you work today as well?"

( )

4. "There is water" is "물이 있어요"
[mu-ri i-sseo-yo.]
Please write "There is water, too" in Korean.

( )

5. Write "Give me this, too" in Korean. There can be two ways.

( )

84

Conjunctions, Tenses,

LESSON **14**

Too, Also

-도 (Part 2)

In the previous lesson, you learned how to use -도 with pronouns and nouns to mean
[-do]

"[noun], too" or "[pronoun] also." Do you remember the formula?

Take a moment to review:

내일 = Tomorrow
[nae-il]
내일도 = Tomorrow, too.
[nae-il-do]

우유 = Milk
[u-yu]
우유도 = Milk, also.
[u-yu-do]

나 = Me
[na]
나도 = Me, too.
[na-do]

물 주세요. = Give me water, please.
[mul ju-se-yo.]
물도 주세요. = Give me water, too, please.
[mul-do ju-se-yo.]

내일 갈 거예요. = I will go tomorrow.
[nae-il gal kkeo-ye-yo.]
내일도 갈 거예요. = I will go (again) tomorrow, too.
[nae-il-do gal kkeo-ye-yo.]

Now that using -도 with nouns and pronouns is fresh in your memory, you can learn how to use -도 with verbs! However, using -도 with verbs as they are is not possible!

Wait. What?!

"How will I learn to use -도 with verbs if it is not possible?"

Well, if you change the verb into its noun form, it is absolutely possible to use -도 with verbs.

Track 27

By changing a verb into its noun form and adding the verb 하다, it literally translates to "to do + verb in noun form + also". It may seem complicated at first, but try to think of -도 하다 as a set when it comes to using -도 with verbs.
[ha-da]

How to change a verb to its noun form

There are a few different ways to change a verb into its noun form, but the simplest and most common way is by adding -기 to the verb stem. This is similar to using verbs in the "to do [verb]" and "[verb]ing" format.
[-gi]

Ex)

보다 = to see
[bo-da]

86

Noun form: 보 + -기 = 보기 (= to do the act of seeing; seeing)
[bo-gi]

보기 → 보기도 하다 = to also see, to even see
[bo-gi-do ha-da]

먹다 = to eat
[meok-tta]
Noun form: 먹 + -기 = 먹기 (= to do the act of eating; eating)
[meok-kki]

먹기 → 먹기도 하다 = to also eat, to even eat
[meok-kki-do ha-da]

잡다 = to catch
[jap-tta]
→ 잡기도 하다 = to also catch; to even catch
[jap-kki-do ha-da]

팔다 = to sell
[pal-da]
→ 팔기도 하다 = to also sell; to even sell
[pal-gi-do ha-da]

Track 27

사다 = to buy
[sa-da]
→ 사기도 하다 = to also buy; to even buy
[sa-gi-do ha-da]

* *Verbs in "noun + 하다" form already (i.e. 공부하다, 청소하다, 노래하다, 준비하다, 요리하다,*
[gong-bu-ha-da], [cheong-so-ha-da], [no-rae-ha-da], [jun-bi-ha-da], [yo-ri-ha-da]
etc.) do not have to be changed in this manner. Just separate the noun from 하다 and add -도
after the noun (i.e. 공부도 하다, 청소도 하다, 노래도 하다, 준비도 하다, 요리도 하다, etc.)

Sample Sentences

저는 영어를 가르쳐요.
[jeo-neun yeong-eo-reul ga-reu-chyeo-yo.]
= I teach English.

저는 영어도 가르쳐요.
[jeo-neun yeong-eo-do ga-reu-chyeo-yo.]
= I teach English as well.

저는 영어를 가르치기도 해요.
[jeo-neun yeong-eo-reul ga-reu-chi-gi-do hae-yo.]

= I also teach English.

= I even teach English.

= I also work as an English teacher.

컴퓨터를 고쳐요.
[keom-pyu-teo-reul go-chyeo-yo.]
= I fix computers.

컴퓨터도 고쳐요.
[keom-pyu-teo-do go-chyeo-yo.]
= I fix computers as well.

컴퓨터를 고치기도 해요.
[keom-pyu-teo-reul go-chi-gi-do hae-yo.]
= I also fix computers.

= I even fix computers.

Track 27

Conjunctions, Tenses,

Sample Dialogue

🎙️ Track 28

A: 여기는 서점이에요, 도서관이에요?
[yeo-gi-neun seo-jeo-mi-e-yo, do-seo-gwa-ni-e-yo?]

B: 서점이에요. 그런데 책을 빌려주기도
해요.
[seo-jeo-mi-e-yo. geu-reon-de chae-geul bil-lyeo-ju-gi-do hae-yo.]

A: 우와!
[u-wa!]

A: Is this place a bookstore or a library?

B: It is a bookstore. However, we also lend out some books.

A: Wow!

Telling Time, and More

✎ Exercises for Lesson 14

Check the answers on **p.197**

1. "To see" is "보다". How do you say "to also see" or "to even see"?

(   )

2. "To sell" is "팔다". How do you write "to also sell" or "to even sell"?

(   )

3. How do you say "I teach English"?

(   )

4. How do you write "I also teach English" or "I even teach English" with focus being on the act of teaching?

(   )

5. "수학" is "mathematics". How do you say "I also teach math" with focus being on the act of
[su-hak]
teaching?

(   )

LESSON 15

Only

$$\boxed{\text{-만}}$$

There are a few different ways to say "only" in Korean, but to prevent your brain from being overloaded, only one of those ways will be covered in this lesson.

Using -만 is one of the most widely used and basic ways of saying "only". Simply add -만 after
[-man]
a noun, pronoun, or noun form (-기) of a verb.
[-gi]

I. Adding -만 after nouns and pronouns

이것 + 만 = 이것만 = only this
[i-geon-man]

    Ex) 이것만 살 거예요. = I will only buy this.
[i-geon-man sal kkeo-ye-yo.]

저 + 만 = 저만 = me only, I only
[jeo-man]
    Ex) 저만 들었어요. = Only I heard.
[jeo-man deu-reo-sseo-yo.]

91

커피 + 만 = 커피만 = only coffee
[keo-pi-man]

Ex) 아침에는 커피만 마셔요. = I drink only coffee in the morning.
[a-chi-me-neun keo-pi-man ma-syeo-yo.]

아침에만 커피(를) 마셔요. = I drink coffee only in the morning.
[a-chi-me-man keo-pi-(reul) ma-syeo-yo.]

2. Adding -만 after noun forms of verbs

** To add -**만** after a verb, change the verb into its noun form using -**기**, then add -**만 하다** which*
[-man ha-da]

literally translates to "only do [noun]".

듣다 = to hear; to listen
[deut-tta]
듣 + 기 = 듣기 = listening (noun form)
[deut-kki]
듣 + -기 + -만 하다 = 듣기만 하다 = to only listen
[deut-kki-man ha-da]

Track 29

Ex) 듣기만 했어요. = I only listened (and did not talk).
[deut-kki-man hae-sseo-yo.]

보다 = to see, to look
[bo-da]
보 + 기 = 보기 = seeing, looking
[bo-gi]
보 + -기 + -만 하다 = 보기만 하다 = to only see, to just look
[bo-gi-man ha-da]

Ex) 보기만 할 거예요. = I will only look (and not touch it).
[bo-gi-man hal kkeo-ye-yo.]

Sample Sentences

오늘만 일찍 왔어요.
[o-neul-man il-jjik wa-sseo-yo.]
= I got here early only today.

오늘 = today

일찍 = early

왔어요. = I came, I got here.

책 한 권만 주문했어요.
[chaek han gwon-man ju-mun-hae-sseo-yo.]
= I only ordered one book.

책 한 권 = one book

주문했어요. = I ordered.

왜 이것만 샀어요?
[wae i-geon-man sa-sseo-yo?]
= Why did you only buy this?

사다 = to buy
[sa-da]
샀어요. = I bought it.

이것 = this, this stuff
[i-geot]
왜 = why

어제 놀기만 했어요.
[eo-je nol-gi-man hae-sseo-yo.]
= I did nothing but play yesterday.

놀다 = to play
[nol-da]
어제 = yesterday

영화는 집에서만 봐요.
[yeong-hwa-neun ji-be-seo-man bwa-yo.]
= I watch movies only at home.

영화 = a movie

집에서 = at home

Track
29

Sample Dialogue

Track 30

A: 왜 책상만 있어요? 의자는 없어요?
[wae chaek-sang-man i-sseo-yo? ui-ja-neun eop-sseo-yo?]

B: 의자도 올 거예요.
[ui-ja-do ol kkeo-ye-yo.]

A: 언제요?
[eon-je-yo?]

B: 내일 올 거예요.
[nae-il ol kkeo-ye-yo.]

A: Why is there only a desk? There's no chair?

B: A chair will come, too.

A: When?

B: It will come tomorrow.

94

✏ *Exercises for Lesson 15*

1. What is the word for "only" which is attached after nouns and pronouns?

( )

2. How do you say "this only"?

( )

3. "To see" is "보다". How do you say "to only see"?

( )

4. How do you write "I only drink coffee"?

( )

5. "To order" is "주문하다". How do you say "I only ordered one book"?
[ju-mu-na-da]

( )

Check the answers on **p.197**

95

LESSON 16

A bit, Really, Very, Not really, Not at all

조금, 정말, 진짜, 아주, 별로, 전혀

Track 31

By the end of this lesson, you will be able to create sentences with stronger emphasis and richer context. You CAN keep your sentences very simple, but being able to add "really", "truly", "a little", "very", or "not really" to emphasize a point can really kick your Korean fluency up a notch!

Please take a look at the following five words and how they are used in Korean sentences:

조금 = a little, a bit, a little bit
[jo-geum]

정말 = really, truly
[jeong-mal]

아주 = very, quite
[a-ju]

별로 = not really, not particularly
[byeol-lo]

전혀 = not at all
[jeo-nyeo]

* 조금, 아주, *and* 정말 *can be used with any sentence, but* 별로 *and* 전혀 *can only be used with negative sentences.*

Conjunctions, Tenses,

<h1 style="text-align:center">조금 = a little, a bit, a little bit</h1>

Sample Sentences

조금 비싸요.
[jo-geum bi-ssa-yo.]
= It is a little expensive.

조금만 주세요.
[jo-geum-man ju-se-yo.]
= Give me only a little bit.

물 조금만 주세요.
[mul jo-geum-man ju-se-yo.]
= Give me only a little bit of water.

Track 31

소금 조금만 주세요.
[so-geum jo-geum-man ju-se-yo.]
= Give me only a little bit of salt.

* When pronounced quickly, 조금 often becomes 좀 (often pronounced like 쫌) and is frequently
[jom]　　　　　　　　　　　　　[jjom]
written this way as well.

** The use of **조금** to mean "quite" or "very" is possible based on the assumption that the other
person in the conversation understands what you mean. For example, in the first sample sentence,
조금 비싸요, can mean both "it is a little expensive" or "it is quite expensive" depending on tone
and context.

정말 = really, truly

Sample Sentences

정말 빨라요.
[ppal-la-yo.]
= It is really fast.

정말 이상해요.
[i-sang-hae-yo.]
= It is really strange.

* A word which has almost the same meaning as 정말 is 진짜. It is considered a little less formal
[jin-jja]
than 정말.

** Whereas other words introduced here are used to describe the extent to which something is

done or to describe the intensity of a certain state (i.e. "very" good, "a little" expensive or "quite"

fast), 정말 and 진짜 can also be used to just express whether or not what is being said is true. (i.e.

I "really" did it).

Sample Conversation

A: 제가 방 청소했어요!
[je-ga bang cheong-so-hae-sseo-yo!]
= I cleaned up my room!

B. 아... 진짜?
[ah...jin-jja?]
= Oh, really?

A: 예, 진짜! 보고 싶어요?
[ye, jin-jja! bo-go si-peo-yo?]
= Yeah, really! Do you want to see it?

아주 = very, quite

Sample Sentences

아주 맛있어요.
[ma-si-sseo-yo.]
= It is very delicious.

아주 멀어요.
[meo-reo-yo.]
= It is very far away.

* 아주 *is the most standard way of saying "very" in the written form, but more often than not, in spoken Korean,* 아주 *is replaced with* 정말 *or* 진짜.

Track 31

별로 = not really; not particularly

* 별로 *is always used in negative sentences, regardless of whether the verb that follows has a negative or a positive meaning.*

** *Rather than just using* 별로, *sometimes, in Korean,* 안 *must be added to the sentence to*
[an]
actually make the sentence a negative. Using 별로 *when speaking will allow the listener to guess that the end of the sentence will be something in negative form.*

Sample Sentences

별로 안 비싸요.
[an bi-ssa-yo.]
= It is not so expensive.

99

별로 재미없어요.
[jae-mi-eop-sseo-yo.]
= It is not that interesting.

* 재미없어요 *is one word, but because* 없어요 *is already within the word itself, it is possible to say* "별로 재미없어요".

별로 안 나빠요.
[an na-ppa-yo.]
= It is not too bad. (It is not the worst, but it is still bad. Note: this does not mean the same thing as the English phrase "it is not bad").

* *Even if the word* 나쁘다 *has a negative meaning, saying only* "별로 나쁘다" *does not work.*
[na-ppeu-da]   [byeol-lo na-ppeu-da]

Track 31

전혀 = not at all

Sample Sentences

전혀 안 바빠요.
[an ba-ppa-yo.]
= I am not busy at all.

전혀 안 더워요.
[an deo-wo-yo.]
= It is not hot at all.

* *In spoken Korean, the expression* 하나도 *is used more commonly than* 전혀.
[ha-na-do]

Sample Dialogue

Track
32

A: 저랑 제 동생이랑 닮았어요?
[jeo-rang je dong-saeng-i-rang dal-ma-sseo-yo?]

B: 아니요, 전혀 안 닮았어요.
[a-ni-yo, jeon-hyeo an dal-ma-sseo-yo.]

A: 저하고 저희 엄마랑은요?
[jeo-ha-go jeo-hui eom-ma-rang-eun-nyo?]

B: 조금 닮았어요.
[jo-geum dal-ma-sseo-yo.]

A: Do my younger sister/brother and I look alike?

B: No. You guys don't look like each other at all.

A: What about my mother and I?

B: You two look a little bit alike.

Telling Time, and More

✎ *Exercises for Lesson* **16**

Translate the following sentences to Korean.

1. "It is a bit expensive."

(   )

2. "It is very interesting."

(   )

3. "It is really strange."

(   )

4. "It is not that expensive."

(   )

5. "It is not interesting at all."

(   )

Check the answers on **p.198**

Conjunctions, Tenses,

LESSON 17

Can, Cannot

-(으)ㄹ 수 있다/없다

When speaking Korean, whether just practicing or speaking out of necessity, there will come a point when knowing how to say "can (do something)" or "cannot (do something)" will come in handy.

To say "can (do something)", use -(으)ㄹ 수 있다
[-(eu)l ssu it-tta]

> ### Conjugation
>
> 보다 = to see
> [bo-da]
> → 보 + -ㄹ 수 있다 = 볼 수 있다 = can see
> [bol ssu it-tta]
>
> 먹다 = to eat
> [meok-tta]
> → 먹 + -을 수 있다 = 먹을 수 있다 = can eat
> [meo-geul ssu it-tta]

* *Verb stems ending in a vowel are followed by* -ㄹ 수 있다, *and verb stems ending with a consonant are followed by* -을 수 있다. *The difference is whether there is an extra* 으 *or not in*

103

front of -ㄹ 수 있다 for the ease of pronunciation.

Regarding -(으)ㄹ 수 있다, the word 수 means an "idea" or "way" for solving a problem or for getting something finished. 수 has the same meaning as 방법 (a method); therefore,
[bang-beop]
-(으)ㄹ 수 있다 literally means "to have a way/idea (for doing something)".

When there is no "way" or "idea" to do something, it means that it cannot be done, and in Korean, this becomes -(으)ㄹ 수 없다. 없다 has the opposite meaning of 있다.
[-(eu)l ssu eop-tta]

Track 33

> ### Conjugation
> 자다 = to sleep
> [ja-da]
> → 자 + -ㄹ 수 없다 = 잘 수 없다 = cannot sleep
> [jal ssu eop-tta]
> ⟷ 잘 수 있다 = can sleep
>
> 잡다 = to catch
> [jap-tta]
> → 잡 + -을 수 없다 = 잡을 수 없다 = cannot catch
> [ja-beul ssu eop-tta]
> ⟷ 잡을 수 있다 = can catch

Another way to say -(으)ㄹ 수 없다 is by using the word 못 before a verb.
[mot]

-(으)ㄹ 수 없다 is the most basic way to express "cannot", but it is not always used in spoken Korean. A more common way to say "cannot" or "to be unable to" in spoken Korean is by adding 못 before a verb.

갈 수 없다 = 못 가다 [verb: 가다] = cannot go
[gal ssu eop-tta]   [mot ga-da]

볼 수 없다 = 못 보다 [verb: 보다] = cannot see

먹을 수 없다 = 못 먹다 [verb: 먹다] = cannot eat

할 수 없다 = 못 하다 [verb: 하다] = cannot do
[hal ssu eop-tta]   [mot ha-da]

Sample Sentences

운전 할 수 있어요?
[un-jeon hal ssu i-sseo-yo?]
= Can you drive? (lit. "Can you do driving?")

일본어 할 수 있어요?
[il-bo-neo hal ssu i-sseo-yo?]
= Can you speak Japanese? (lit. "Can you do Japanese?")

Track 33

이거 읽을 수 있어요?
[i-geo il-geul ssu i-sseo-yo?]
= Can you read this?

못 읽어요.
[mot il-geo-yo.]
= I cannot read it.

지금 못 만나요.
[ji-geum mot man-na-yo.]
= I cannot meet you now.

Sample Dialogue

Track
34

A: 미경 씨, 기타 칠 수 있어요?
[mi-gyeong ssi, gi-ta chil ssu i-sseo-yo?]

B: 아니요. 그런데 곧 배울 거예요.
경화 씨는요?
[a-ni-yo. geu-reon-de got bae-ul kkeo-ye-yo.
gyeong-hwa ssi-neun-nyo?]

A: 저도 배울 거예요.
[jeo-do bae-ul kkeo-ye-yo.]

A: Mikyung, can you play the guitar?

B: No, but I am going to learn soon.
How about you, Kyung-hwa?

A: I am going to learn, too.

Conjunctions, Tenses,

✎ Exercises for Lesson 17

1. "To go" is "가다". How do you say "I can go"?
[ga-da]

( )

2. How do you say "I can't do it"?

( )

3. Please write "Can you do this?"

( )

4. Please write "Can we meet now?"

( )

5. "To swim" is "수영하다". Please write "Can you swim?"
[su-yeong-ha-da]

( )

Check the answers on **p.198**

LESSON **18**

To be good/poor at ···

잘하다, 못하다

Track 35

In Lesson 17, you learned how to say "can" or "cannot" in Korean. Take that knowledge one step further by learning how to construct sentences to express that you are "good" or "bad" at doing something.

> ### *Conjugation*
>
> [object] + -을/를 (object marking particle) + 잘하다
> [-eul/reul]   [jal-ha-da]
> = to do [object] well; to be good at [object]
>
>
> [object] + -을/를 + 못하다
>   [mo-ta-da]
> = to do [object] poorly; to be bad at [object]

Ex)

노래 = singing; song
[no-rae]
노래를 잘하다 = to be good at singing; to sing well

요리 = cooking, dish
[yo-ri]
요리를 못하다 = to be poor at cooking; to cook poorly

* Saying 못 하다 with a pause or space between 못 and 하다 gives the phrase the meaning of
[mot ha-da]
"to be unable to do (something)" or "cannot do (something)".

** 잘 is often added in front of 못하다 to make the meaning softer. By saying 잘 못하다, the
[jal]
meaning is literally "cannot do (something) well" or "unable to do (something) well".

요리를 못하다 = to be poor at cooking
요리를 잘 못하다 = to be poor at cooking

Ex)

수영 = swimming
[su-yeong]
수영을 잘하다 = to be good at swimming
[su-yeong-eul jal-ha-da]
수영을 못하다 = to be bad at swimming
[su-yeong-eul mo-ta-da]
수영을 잘 못하다 = to be bad at swimming
[su-yeong-eul jal mo-ta-da]

Track 35

* *IMPORTANT: Be very careful when saying* 잘 못하다. *Saying this phrase with a pause between*
잘 *and* 못, 잘 못하다, *gives the meaning "to be poor at (something)". Not placing a pause*
between 잘 *and* 못, *as in* 잘못 하다 *gives the impression of "to do (something) in the wrong*
[jal-mot ha-da]
way". Additionally, saying 잘못하다 *with no pause between any of the words means "to make a*
[jal-mo-ta-da]
mistake".

Are 잘 and 못 (or 잘 못) only used with -하다 verbs?

No. Other types of verbs can be used with 잘 and 못 as well. Since the first part of most
-하다 verbs are nouns, it is easy to detach the noun from -하다 and add 잘, 못, or 잘 못 in

109

front of -하다. For other types of verbs which are not in the "noun + -하다" form, just add 잘, 못, or 잘 못 in front of the verb with a space in between.

잘 달리다 = to run well, to be good at running
[dal-li-da]
잘 쓰다 = to write well, to be good at writing
[sseu-da]

When a verb is used on its own, however, often times the meaning is not very clear. For example, 쓰다 can mean both "to write" and "to use". The phrase sounds incomplete with only using a verb; therefore, a noun is added to the phrase to give the verb a more specific meaning.

잘 쓰다 → 글을 잘 쓰다 (= to be good at writing; to be a good writer)
[geu-reul]
[lit. "to write well"]

Track 35

글 is a noun meaning "written text", "a piece of writing", or "a composition".
[geul]

잘 쓰다 → 글씨를 잘 쓰다 (= to be good at handwriting; to have good penmanship)
[geul-ssi-reul]
[lit. "to write writing/letters well"]

Here, the word 글씨, meaning "writing" or "letters", is used to make the meaning of "writing" clearer and prevent people from thinking that it might mean "to use".

잘 달리다 → 달리기를 잘하다 (= to be good at running)
[dal-li-gi-reul]
[lit. "to do running well"]

달리다 was changed to its noun form here and followed by 잘하다.

Sample Sentences

저는 노래를 잘 못해요.
[jeo-neun no-rae-reul jal mo-tae-yo.]
= I cannot sing well. / I am not good at singing.

제 친구는 수영을 잘해요.
[je chin-gu-neun su-yeong-eul jal-hae-yo.]
= My friend is good at swimming.

저는 퍼즐을 잘 풀어요.
[jeo-neun peo-jeu-reul jal pu-reo-yo.]
= I am good at solving puzzles.

저는 글씨를 잘 못 써요.
[jeo-neun geul-ssi-reul jal mot sseo-yo.]
= My handwriting is not good.

Track 35

저는 글을 잘 못 써요.
[jeo-neun geu-reul jal mot sseo-yo.]
= I am not good at writing.

매운 거 잘 먹어요?
[mae-un geo jal meo-geo-yo?]
= Are you good at eating spicy food?

Sample Dialogue

A: 경은 씨는 요리 잘해요?
[gyeong-eun ssi-neun yo-ri jal-hae-yo?]

B: 아니요, 잘 못해요. 석진 씨는요?
[a-ni-yo, jal mo-tae-yo. seok-jjin ssi-neun-nyo?]

A: 저도 잘 못해요.
[jeo-do jal mo-tae-yo.]

A: Are you a good cook, Kyeong-eun?

B: No, not really. How about you, Seokjin?

A: I am not good at it either.

Conjunctions, Tenses,

✎ *Exercises for Lesson 18*

1. "To do" is "하다". How do you say "to do something well" or "to be good at doing something"?

( )

2. How do you write "to be bad at doing something"?

( )

3. What can you say to imply that you cannot do something or are unable to do something?

( )

4. Write "I am good at swimming" in Korean.

( )

5. How do you say "I am not good at singing"?

( )

Check the answers on **p.198**

Telling Time, and More

LESSON 19

Making Verbs Into Nouns

-는 것

Track 37

In Level 2, Lesson 14, you learned how to add the meaning of "also" in Korean by adding -도 to a verb. In order to do this, however, the verb needs to be changed into its noun form [-do]
by adding -기 to the verb stem, then add -도, and end with 하다. (Is it all coming back to you [-gi]   [ha-da]
now?)

In this lesson, you will expand that knowledge by looking at a more general way of making action verbs into nouns. Understanding this will help your understanding of how to form a number of expressions in Korean.

-는 것

This is the most general way of changing an action verb into a noun. 것 originally means "a thing", "an object", or "stuff", but when it is used in this way, it can also mean "a fact" or "an act".

114

Conjugation

- Verb stem + -는 것
[-neun geot]

By changing verbs into nouns, the form [verb stem + -는 것] can take many different meanings:

1. "doing" something

2. the act of "doing" something

3. the thing which one "does"

4. what one "does"

5. the fact that one is "doing" or "does" something

Ex)

보다 = to see
[bo-da]

보는 것 = seeing; the act of seeing; the thing which one sees; what one watches
[bo-neun geot]

가다 = to go
[ga-da]

가는 것 = going; the act of going
[ga-neun geot]

먹다 = to eat
[meok-tta]

먹는 것 = eating; the act of eating; the thing which one eats; what one eats
[meog-neun geot]

사다 = to buy
[sa-da]

사는 것 = buying; the act of buying; the thing which one buys; what one buys
[sa-neun geot]

산 것 = what one bought
[san-geot]

사는 것 = what one buys

살 것 = what one will buy
[sal geot]

먹은 것 = what one ate
[meo-geun geot]

먹는 것 = what one eats

먹을 것 = what one will eat
[meo-geul geot]

-는 것 vs. -는 거

-는 것 is the standard form, but often at times the form -는 거 is used because it is easier to
pronounce. It is not, however, ever used in very formal situations.
[-neun geo]

지금 듣는 것은 노래예요.
[ji-geum deun-neun geo-seun no-rae-ye-yo.]
= What I am listening to now is a song.

→ 지금 듣는 거는 노래예요.

오늘 만나는 것 알아요?
[o-neul man-na-neun geot a-ra-yo?]
= Do you know that we are meeting today?

→ 오늘 만나는 거 알아요?

**Track
37**

매운 것 잘 먹어요?
[mae-un geot jal meo-geo-yo?]
= Are you good at eating spicy food?

→ 매운 거 잘 먹어요?

Sample Sentences

제 취미는 영화 보는 거예요.
[je chwi-mi-neun yeong-hwa bo-neun geo-ye-yo.]
= My hobby is watching movies.

요즘 공부하는 거는 뭐예요?
[yo-jeum gong-bu-ha-neun geo-neun mwo-ye-yo?]
= Recently, what is it that you are studying?

= 요즘 뭐 공부해요?

저는 친구랑 수다 떠는 거를 좋아해요.
[jeo-neun chin-gu-rang su-da tteo-neun geo-reul jo-a-hae-yo.]
= I like chitchatting with my friends.

Sample Dialogue

Track 38

A: 남편한테 말했어요?
[nam-pyeo-nan-te ma-rae-sseo-yo?]

B: 뭐를요?
[mwo-reul-lyo?]

A: 밖에서 저녁 먹는 거요.
[ba-kke-seo jeo-nyeok meong-neun geo-yo.]

B: 네, 말했어요.
[ne, ma-rae-sseo-yo.]

A: Have you told your husband?

B: What do you mean?

A: That you were going out to have dinner.

B: Yes, I told him.

✎ Exercises for Lesson 19

1. "To eat" is "먹다". How do you write "eating", "the act of eating", or "what one eats" in Korean?

( )

2. "To go" is "가다". How do you say "going" or "the act of going" in Korean?

( )

3. Please write "I like reading books".

( )

4. How do you say "I do not like spicy things"?

( )

5. How do you write "My hobby is watching movies"?

( )

Check the answers on **p.198**

LESSON 20

Have to, Should, Must

-아/어/여야 되다/하다

Track 39

By the end of this lesson, you will be constructing sentences using -아/어/여 + -야 되다/하
[-a/eo/yeo]   [-ya doe-da/ha-da]
다 to say things such as "I have to go to work" or "You should buy it".

To use this ending, take the verb stem and add -아/어/여 PLUS -야 되다 or -야 하다.

> ### Conjugation
> verb stem + -아/어/여 + -야 되다/하다

Ex)

자다 = to sleep
[ja-da]

자 + -아/어/여 + -야 되다/하다

→ 자 + -아 + -야 되다/하다

    (-아 is chosen because 자 ends with a vowel.)

→ 자야 되다/하다 (Drop the -아 because it is the same as ㅏ.)
  [ja-ya doe-da/ha-da]

→ 자야 되다 and 자야 하다 are the same thing.

120

쓰다 = to use; to write
[sseu-da]

쓰 + -아/어/여 + -야 되다/하다

→ 쓰 + -어 + -야 되다/하다

   (-어 is chosen because 쓰 does not end in ㅏ or ㅗ.)

→ 써야 되다/하다 (쓰 + 어 together change to 써)
[sseo-ya doe-da/ha-da]

→ 써야 되다 and 써야 하다 mean the same thing.

> ## Conjugation
> 1. verb stems ending in vowels ㅏ or ㅗ + -아야 되다/하다
> 2. verb stems ending in other vowels + -어야 되다/하다
> 3. 하 + -여야 되다/하다

However, it is more important to understand WHY -아/어/여야 되다/하다 means "to have to" or "should".

To understand this better, look at the two parts separately:

1. -아/어/여 + -야
This means "only when _____ is done" or "only when you do _____".

2. 되다 or 하다
되다 means "to be done" or "to be possible", and 하다 means "to do" something.

Therefore, when putting 1 and 2 together, it takes the meaning of "only when you do _____, it works", "only when you do this, everything is alright", or "only if _____ is done, it is okay". Thus, -아/어/여야 되다/하다 takes the meaning of "to have to" or "should".

121

Q : What is the difference between 하다 and 되다 here?

A : The only difference is that using 되다 is more common in colloquial situations.

Sample Sentences

집에 가야 돼요.
[ji-be ga-ya dwae-yo.]
= I have to go home.

저는 뭐 해야 돼요?
[jeo-neun mwo hae-ya dwae-yo?]
= What should I do?

Track 39

언제까지 여기에 있어야 돼요?
[eon-je-kka-ji yeo-gi-e i-sseo-ya dwae-yo?]
= Until when should I be here?

누구한테 줘야 돼요?
[nu-gu-han-te jwo-ya dwae-yo?]
= Who should I give this to?

어디에서 사야 돼요?
[eo-di-e-seo sa-ya dwae-yo?]
= Where should I buy it?

Sample Dialogue

Track 40

A: 지금 뭐 하고 있어요?
[ji-geum mwo ha-go i-sseo-yo?]

B: 숙제하고 있어요. 내일까지 해야 돼요.
[suk-jje-ha-go i-sseo-yo. nae-il-kka-ji hae-ya dwae-yo.]

A: 내일 몇 시까지 해야 돼요?
[nae-il myeot si-kka-ji hae-ya dwae-yo?]

B: 내일 10시까지 해야 돼요.
[nae-il yeol-si-kka-ji hae-ya dwae-yo.]

A: What are you doing now?

B: I am doing my homework. I have to finish it by tomorrow.

A: By what time tomorrow do you have to finish it?

B: I have to finish it by 10 o'clock tomorrow.

123

Telling Time, and More

✏ Exercises for Lesson **20**

1. What is the difference between 하다 and 되다?

( )

Translate the following to Korean:

2. "I have to go."

( )

3. "I have to write" or "I have to use".

( )

4. "I have to do it now."

( )

5. "Where do you have to go tomorrow?"

( )

Check the answers on **p.198**

Conjunctions, Tenses,

KIMCHI
FRIED RICE

김치 볶음밥 is super delicious, super easy to make, and it fries up so quickly that you'll barely have time to say "한국 음식 진짜 좋아해요!" (I really like Korean food!) before it's cooked!

One of the best things about Korean cooking is that you can add your own flair to it. If you want to add corn, do it! Want to add SPAM or 두부 (tofu)? Go ahead!

This is a pretty basic recipe for 김치 볶음밥, and it makes 2 very generous servings.

Let's get cooking!

You will need:

- 후라이팬 (fry pan)
- 2 cups (or 2 rice bowls) of cooked 밥 (rice)
- 1 cup of 김치 (kimchi) - do not drain or squeeze the liquid!
- ½ of a 양파 (onion)
- 1 clove of 마늘 (garlic)
- 1-2 teaspoons of 고추장 (gochujang – a.k.a. hot pepper paste: 1 tablespoon if you like it medium-hot, and 2 tablespoons if you'd like a death sentence).
- 1 tablespoon of 간장 (soy sauce)
- 2 teaspoons of 설탕 (sugar)
- 2 tablespoons of 김치 juice from the jar
- 2 달걀 (egg)
- 1 teaspoon of 참기름 (sesame oil)
- 2 tablespoons of oil for frying (vegetable, canola, olive etc).
- 깨소금 (sesame seeds) for garnish
- 1 파 (green onion) for garnish

Directions

1. Chop 파, mince 1 clove of 마늘, roughly chop 1 cup of 김치, and cut 양파. Set aside.

2. Heat 1 tablespoon of oil in the 후라이팬 over medium heat.

3. Once the oil is heated, fry the 2 달걀. Traditionally, the 달걀 is served sunny-side up.

(* Note: You can cook the 달걀 before you start to cook the rice, or you can cook it after you've plated the rice and wiped the 후라이팬 clean, or you can cook the 달걀 in a separate 후라이팬. Basically, you can cook the 달걀 whenever you want and however you want!)

4. Heat the remaining 1 tablespoon of oil in the 후라이팬.

5. When the oil is heated, add 마늘 and 양파. Sauté until you can smell them (about 1 minute).

6. Add chopped 김치. Fry for 2-3 minutes.

7. Add 밥 and stir well to combine.

8. Turn down the heat (medium-low) and add 김치 juice, 간장, 설탕, and 고추장.

9. Stir/fold to make sure it mixes well with the rice.

10. Turn off the heat and add 1 teaspoon of 참기름. Mix well.

11. Put the 김치 볶음밥 on a plate or in a bowl and put a fried egg on top. Garnish with 깨소금 and chopped 파!

Voilà! Delicious 김치 볶음밥!

You are half way finished with Level 2!
Cook up some 김치 볶음밥 *to replenish*
your strength and power through the rest of this book!

LESSON **21**

more ··· than ···

-보다 더

After studying with this lesson, you will be able to compare two things or people in Korean by saying that something is better/taller/faster/prettier/nicer/etc. than something else.

How to say "more" in Korean

In Korean, the word for "more" is 더. In English, relatively short words change forms instead
[deo]
of having the word "more" in front, such as "shorter", "hotter", and "faster". In Korean, however, all words just have 더 in front of them.

Ex)

빠르다 = to be fast
[ppa-reu-da]
더 빠르다 = to be faster
[deo ppa-reu-da]

비싸다 = to be expensive
[bi-ssa-da]
더 비싸다 = to be more expensive
[deo bi-ssa-da]

130

예뻐요. = It is pretty. / You are pretty. / She is pretty.
[ye-ppeo-yo.]

더 예뻐요. = It is prettier. / You are prettier. / She is prettier.
[deo ye-ppeo-yo.]

How to say "than" in Korean

The word for "than" or "compared to" is -보다. The basic construction for this is not very
[-bo-da]
complicated, but the word order in Korean is completely different from English. Take a look
at the following example:

English: A watermelon is bigger than an apple.

Korean: 수박은 사과보다 더 커요.
[su-ba-geun sa-gwa-bo-da deo keo-yo.]

* *In the English sentence above, the word "than" comes BEFORE "apple", but in Korean, the word*
-보다 (which means "than") comes AFTER 사과, which means "apple".

Track 41

> *Conjugation*
>
> than A = A보다
>
> more (verb/adjective/adverb) than A = A보다 더 (verb/adjective/adverb)

Ex)

(1) to be big = 크다
[keu-da]

　to be bigger = 더 크다
[deo keu-da]

　It is bigger. = 더 커요.
[deo keo-yo.]

　It is bigger than this one. = 이거보다 더 커요.
[i-geo-bo-da deo keo-yo.]

(2) to be nice = 좋다
[jo-ta]

　to be nicer = 더 좋다
[deo jo-ta]

131

It is nicer. = 더 좋아요.
[deo jo-a-yo.]

It is nicer than this one. = 이거보다 더 좋아요.
[i-geo-bo-da deo jo-a-yo.]

(3) to be nice (to people) = 착하다
[cha-ka-da]

to be nicer = 더 착하다
[deo cha-ka-da]

Hyunwoo is nicer. = 현우 씨는 더 착해요.
[hyeo-nu ssi-neun deo cha-kae-yo.]

Hyunwoo is nicer than Kyeong-eun. = 현우 씨는 경은 씨보다 더 착해요.
[hyeo-nu ssi-neun gyeong-eun ssi-bo-da deo cha-kae-yo.]

* 더 *is not always necessary in Korean. Saying "she is busy than me" instead of "she is busier than me" in English is a bit weird, but in Korean, the meaning is perfectly clear even without the word* 더.

Track 41

Sample Sentences

오늘은 어제보다 더워요.
[o-neu-reun eo-je-bo-da deo-wo-yo.]
= Today is hotter than yesterday.

영어는 한국어보다 어려워요.
[yeong-eo-neun han-gu-geo-bo-da eo-ryeo-wo-yo.]
= English is more difficult than Korean.

어제보다 일찍 갈 거예요.
[eo-je-bo-da il-jjik gal kkeo-ye-yo.]
= I am going to go earlier than yesterday.

현정 씨가 저보다 더 잘해요.
[hyeon-jeong ssi-ga jeo-bo-da deo ja-rae-yo.]
= Hyeonjeong is better than me (at doing that).

저는 책을 읽는 것보다 사는 것을 더 좋아해요.
[jeo-neun chae-geul ing-neun geot-bo-da saneun geo-seul deo jo-a-hae-yo.]
= I like buying books more than reading books.

132

Sample Dialogue

Track 42

A: 어제보다 오늘 손님이 더 많았어요?
[eo-je-bo-da o-neul son-ni-mi deo ma-na-sseo-yo?]

B: 아니요. 오늘보다 어제가 더 많았어요.
[a-ni-yo. o-neul-bo-da eo-je-ga deo ma-na-sseo-yo.]

A: 아, 그래요?
[a, geu-rae-yo?]

A: Were there more customers today than there were yesterday?

B: No. There were more customers yesterday than there were today.

A: Oh, there were?

133

🖉 Exercises for Lesson 21

Check the answers on **p.198**

1. "To be fast" is "빠르다". How do you write "to be faster"?

(   )

2. "To be good" is "좋다". How do you say "to be better"?

(   )

3. Please write "Coffee is more expensive than water".

(   )

4. How do you say "This book is more interesting than that book over there"?

(   )

5. How do you write "I came here earlier than yesterday"?

(   )

Conjunctions, Tenses,

LESSON **22**

To like

좋다 vs. 좋아하다

A verb which is often encountered in Korean is **좋다**, which generally means "to be good".

However, there are a few instances where **좋다** takes on the meaning of "to like".
[jo-ta]

Track 43

Ex)

한국어 좋아요.
[han-gu-geo jo-a-yo.]
= I like the Korean language.

이거 좋아요.
[i-geo jo-a-yo.]
= I like this.

이 가수 좋아요.
[i ga-su]
= I like this singer.

Even though the verb **좋다** in these examples is used to mean "to like", the dictionary definition of the verb is "to be good". In principle, the nouns (한국어, 이거, 이 가수) are subjects of the sentences.

Therefore, the particles which are hidden after the nouns are NOT object marking particles, but in fact, are subject marking particles.

한국어 좋아요.
→ 한국어를 좋아요. (x)
  [han-gu-geo-reul jo-a-yo.]
→ 한국어가 좋아요. (o)
  [han-gu-geo-ga jo-a-yo.]

In this sentence, you are literally saying that "Korean is good, likable, enjoyable, and preferable" FOR YOU.

Track 43

The difference between 좋다 and 좋아하다

한국어 좋아해요.
  [jo-a-hae-yo.]
→ 한국어를 좋아해요. (o)
→ 한국어가 좋아해요. (x)

By dropping the particles, there is no difference between 좋다 and 좋아하다.
  [jo-a-ha-da]

(1) 이 가수 좋아요.
(2) 이 가수 좋아해요.

Sentences (1) and (2) have the same meaning - "This singer is good" or "I like this singer". To specify what is good and who likes whom, adding particles is recommended.

(3) 이 가수가 좋아요.
   [i ga-su-ga]
(4) 이 가수를 좋아요.
   [i ga-su-reul]

Sentence number (3) means that you like this singer, however sentence number (4) is not correct because 좋다 is a descriptive verb and cannot have an object.

(5) 이 가수를 좋아해요.
(6) 이 가수가 좋아해요.

Track 43

Sentence number (5) means that you like (or someone else likes) this singer; this singer is the OBJECT of your affection. The SUBJECT of sentence (6) is this singer, and the sentence is translated as "This singer likes". Left as it is, the sentence is incomplete, and what/who this singer likes (OBJECT) needs to be added.

Descriptive verbs + 하다 combination

> *Conjugation*
> Verb stem + -아/어/여 + -하다

As in the case of 좋다 and 좋아하다, there can be many pairs of words which seem similar at first but are actually different in usage.

Ex)

(1) 싫다 / 싫어요.
[sil-ta] [si-reo-yo.]
= to be unlikable; to be undesirable

싫어하다 / 싫어해요.
[si-reo-ha-da] [si-reo-hae-yo.]
= to hate; to not like

(2) 예쁘다 / 예뻐요.
[ye-ppeu-da] [ye-ppeo-yo.]
= to be pretty; to be cute

예뻐하다 / 예뻐해요.
[ye-ppeo-ha-da] [ye-ppeo-hae-yo.]
= to consider someone pretty and treat them in such a manner

(3) 슬프다 / 슬퍼요.
[seul-peu-da] [seul-peo-yo.]
= to be sad

Track 43

슬퍼하다 / 슬퍼해요.
[seul-peo-ha-da] [seul-peo-hae-yo.]
= to feel sad, and therefore, express such emotions

In order to say "don't be sad" or "don't hate me", use -지 마세요 after the verb stem.
[-ji ma-se-yo]
However, "sad" (슬프다) and "hate" (싫다) in Korean are actually descriptive verbs, not
action verbs. To use -지 마세요, descriptive verbs must be made into action verbs by adding
-하다.

Ex)

Don't be sad. = 슬퍼하지 마세요. (o) 슬프지 마세요. (x)
[seul-peo-ha-ji ma-se-yo.]   [seul-peu-ji ma-se-yo.]
Don't hate me. = 싫어하지 마세요. (o) 싫지 마세요. (x)
[si-reo-ha-ji ma-se-yo.]   [sil-chi ma-se-yo.]

Sample Sentences

저는 우유를 좋아해요.
[jeo-neun u-yu-reul jo-a-hae-yo.]
= I like milk.

저는 우유를 안 좋아해요.
[jeo-neun u-yu-reul an jo-a-hae-yo.]
= I do not like milk.

우유가 좋아요? 주스가 좋아요?
[u-yu-ga jo-a-yo? ju-seu-ga jo-a-yo?]
= Do you like milk? Or do you like juice?

뭐가 제일 좋아요?
[mwo-ga je-il jo-a-yo?]
= What is your favorite?

Track 43

뭐를 제일 좋아해요?
[mwo-reul je-il jo-a-hae-yo?]
= What do you like best?

* Here, another difference between 좋다 and 좋아하다 is that 좋다 is used to mean "to like" only about yourself, not about other people. If you want to say "Kyeong-eun likes coffee", use the verb 좋아하다.

Ex) 경은 씨는 커피를 좋아해요.
[gyeong-eun ssi-neun keo-pi-reul jo-a-hae-yo.]

한국 영화 좋아하세요?
[han-guk yeong-hwa jo-a-ha-se-yo?]
= Do you like Korean movies?

Sample Dialogue

A: 한국 드라마 좋아해요?
[han-guk deu-ra-ma jo-a-hae-yo?]

B: 아니요. 저는 드라마 잘 안 봐요.
[a-ni-yo. jeo-neun deu-ra-ma jal an bwa-yo.]

A: 한국 영화는요?
[han-guk yeong-hwa-neun-nyo?]

B: 영화는 좋아해요.
[yeong-hwa-neun jo-a-hae-yo.]

A: Do you like Korean dramas?

B: No. I don't really watch dramas.

A: What about Korean movies?

B: I do like movies.

✏ *Exercises for Lesson* **22**

1. "좋다" and "좋아하다" are similar in meaning but quite different in usage. Which one is closer to "actively" liking something?

(   )

2. Use the verb "좋다" to write "I like the Korean language."

(   )

3. Use the verb "좋아하다" to say "I like the Korean language."

(   )

4. Using the verb "좋아하다", how do you say "민수 likes milk"?

(   )

5. Using the verb "좋다", how do you say "What is your favorite?"

(   )

Check the answers on **p.198**

LESSON 23

If, In case

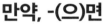

만약, -(으)면

Track 45

After studying with this lesson, you will know how to say "if" in Korean. You will also be able to use it in context in your Korean sentences.

In order to express the meaning "if", you need to know two expressions: one is a noun, and one is a verb ending.

만약 = in case, if

-(으)면 = verb ending for "if"

In English, the word "if" is used at the beginning of a sentence to make the sentence conditional, but in Korean, you can add the word 만약, but you also need to conjugate
[ma-nyak]
the verb as well to match. Do not worry, though! Conjugating verbs in this manner is very straightforward.

How to conjugate verbs

In order to add the meaning "if" to a verb, add -(으)면 to the verb stem.
[-(eu)-myeon]

> ### *Conjugation*
>
> 1. **Verb stems ending with a vowel + -면**
>
>   **Ex)** 자다 → 자면 (if you sleep)
>   [ja-da]   [ja-myeon]
>
> 2. **Verb stems ending with ㄹ + -면**
>
>   **Ex)** 길다 → 길면 (if it is long)
>   [gil-da]   [gil-myeon]
>
> 3. **Verb stems ending with consonants other than ㄹ + -으면**
>
>   **Ex)** 작다 → 작으면 (if it is small)
>   [jak-tta]   [ja-geu-myeon]

**Track
45**

To make the sentence clearer, add the word 만약 in front of the verb or at the beginning of the phrase. Since most Korean sentences are heavily affected by verb endings toward the end of sentences, adding 만약 at the beginning makes it easier to understand that the sentence will be conditional.

Ex)

(1) Verb: 자다 = to sleep

지금 자면 = if I sleep now
[ji-geum]
만약 지금 자면 = if I sleep now

(2) Verb: 비가 오다 = to rain
[bi-ga- o-da]
내일 밤에 비가 오면 = if it rains tomorrow night
[nae-il ba-me]
만약 내일 밤에 비가 오면 = if it rains tomorrow night

* In the second sentences for both examples on the previous page, the listener can figure out that the sentence is going to be an "if" sentence just by hearing "만약".

If what you are saying is simple and the sentence is not very long, you do not always have to use the word 만약 in each sentence.

More Examples

먹다 = to eat
[meok-tta]
먹으면 = if you eat it; if I eat it
[meo-geu-myeon]

Track 45

* Add the -았/었/였- suffix before -으면 to make a past tense clause.
[-at/eot/yeot-]

먹었어요 = I ate
[meo-geo-sseo-yo]
먹 + 었 + 으면 = if you ate it; if I ate it
[meo-geo-sseu-myeon]

사다 = to buy
[sa-da]
사면 = if you buy it; if I buy it; if they buy it
[sa-myeon]
샀어요 = I bought
[sa-sseo-yo]
샀으면 = if you bought it; if we bought it
[sa-sseu-myeon]

* Create future tense sentences by using -(으)ㄹ 거면.
[-(eu)l kkeo-myeon]

보다 = to watch
[bo-da]
보면 = if you watch it; if I watch it
[bo-myeon]
봤어요 = I watched
[bwa-sseo-yo]

봤으면 = if I watched it; if they watched it
[bwa-sseu-myeon]
볼 거예요 = I am going to watch
[bol kkeo-ye-yo]
볼 거면 = if you are going to watch it
[bol geo-myeon]

Sample Sentences

내일 비가 오면, 집에 있을 거예요.
[nae-il bi-ga o-myeon, ji-be i-sseul kkeo-ye-yo.]
= If it rains tomorrow, I am going to be at home.

이거 다 먹으면, 배가 아플 거예요.
[i-geo da meo-geu-myeon, bae-ga a-peul kkeo-ye-yo.]
= If you eat all of it, your stomach will hurt.

리모컨을 찾으면, TV를 볼 수 있어요.
[ri-mo-keo-neul cha-jeu-myeon, ti-bi-reul bol su i-sseo-yo.]
= If you find the remote control, you can watch TV.

Track 45

TTMIK으로* 공부하면, 재미있어요.
[TTMIK-eu-ro gong-bu-ha-myeon, jae-mi-i-sseo-yo.]
= If you study with TTMIK, it is fun.   *p. 173

지금 안 오면, 후회할 거예요.
[ji-geum an o-myeon hu-hoe-hal kkeo-ye-yo.]
= If you do not come now, you will regret it.

This is not everything.

This is, however, one of the most basic and frequently used ways to make "if" sentences in Korean. There are other expressions which can be used, but those will have to wait until future lessons to be introduced. In the meantime, enjoy practicing what you learned with us in this lesson!

Sample Dialogue

A: 그거 사지 마세요.
[geu-geo sa-ji ma-se-yo.]

B: 왜요?
[wae-yo?]

A: 다른 곳에서 사면 더 싸요.
[da-reun go-se-seo sa-myeon deo ssa-yo.]

A: Don't buy that.

B: Why not?

A: It is cheaper if you buy it at another place.

✏️ Exercises for Lesson 23

1. If "to sleep" is "자다" in Korean, how do you say "If I sleep now"?

( )

Match the Korean word to its English equivalent.

2. 보다

a. if you are going to watch it

3. 보면

b. if you watch it, if I watch it

4. 봤으면

c. to watch

5. 볼 거면

d. if I watched it, if they watched it

6. Write the following sentence in Korean: "If it rains tomorrow, I am going to be at home."

( )

Check the answers on **p.198**

147

LESSON **24**

Still, Already

아직, 벌써

**Track
47**

The focus of this lesson is on two new expressions with opposite meanings, which can help you express "still" or "not yet" and "already".

아직 means "still" and "not yet".

In English, generally, the word "still" is used with positive sentences, and the word "yet" is more commonly used with negative sentences. However, in Korean, the word 아직 is used
[a-jik]
for both positive and negative sentences.

아직 10시예요.
[yeol-ssi-ye-yo.]
= It is still 10 o'clock.

아직 안 했어요.
[an hae-sseo-yo.]
= I have not done it yet.

148

Conjunctions, Tenses,

아직 아침이에요.
[a-chi-mi-e-yo.]
= It is still morning.

아직 몰라요.
[mol-la-yo.]
= I do not know yet.

To emphasize the meaning of "still happening" or "still not happening", add the particle -도
[-do]
after 아직 to form 아직도. 아직도 has a meaning of criticizing the other person or being a
[a-jik-tto]
little bit mad or angry.

아직 몰라요?

= You do not know yet?

아직도 몰라요?
[a-jik-tto]
= You still do not know? / How could you still not know?

아직 안 왔어요?
[an wa-sseo-yo?]
= He is not here yet?

아직도 안 왔어요?

= He is still not here yet?

네, 아직도 안 왔어요.
[ne]
= No, he is still not here.

벌써 means "already".

The usage of the word 벌써 is very similar to the English word "already". It is generally placed
[beol-sseo]
at the beginning of sentences, but it does not always have to be at the beginning.

It is already three o'clock.

= 벌써 세 시예요.
[se si-ye-yo.]

It is three o'clock already!

= 세 시예요, 벌써!

**Track
47**

Both of the sentences above are correct.

Sample Sentences

벌써 왔어요?
[beol-sseo wa-sseo-yo?]
= Oh, you are already here!

벌써 끝났어요.
[beol-sseo kkeun-na-sseo-yo..]
= It is already over.

벌써 끝났어요?
[beol-sseo kkeun-na-sseo-yo?]
= Is it already over? Did it already finish?

150

이미 vs. 벌써

Another word which also has the meaning of "already" is 이미. You will probably come across this word frequently when reading or listening to Korean.
[i-mi]

Although 벌써 and 이미 appear to have the same meaning, native speakers often distinguish the two by using them in different contexts.

The difference between 이미 and 벌써 lies in whether you are already aware of a fact or not. When you and/or the speaker know about something already and talk about it, use 이미. When you are just finding out about something as you speak, use 벌써. People do not always stick to this rule, but this is the basic idea.

Track 47

> **Ex)**
> 그 사람은 이미 학교를 졸업했어요.
> [geu sa-ra-meun i-mi hak-kkyo-reul jo-reo-pae-sseo-yo.]
> = He already graduated from school.

- You (and probably the other person) have known about this long before you said this sentence.

그 사람은 벌써 학교를 졸업했어요!
= He already graduated from school.

- You may have found out about this fact recently, or you already knew about this, but the other person may have not known about it before you said it.

Because of this difference, in normal everyday situations where new information is discovered, 벌써 is used.

벌써 비가 오고 있어요.
[bi-ga o-go i-sseo-yo.]
= It is already raining.

벌써 추워요.
[chu-wo-yo.]
= It is already cold.

벌써 끝났어요.

= It is already over.

Track 47

Sample Dialogue

Track 48

A: 경화 씨, 집이에요?
[gyeong-hwa ssi, ji-bi-e-yo?]

B: 아니요. 아직 사무실이에요.
[a-ni-yo. a-jik sa-mu-si-ri-e-yo.]

A: 아직도요? 지금 밤 10시예요!
[a-jik-tto-yo? ji-geum bam yeol-ssi-ye-yo!]

B: 벌써요?
[beol-sseo-yo?]

A: *Kyung-hwa, are you home?*

B: *No. I am still at my office.*

A: *Still? It is 10PM!*

B: *Already?*

Telling Time, and More

✎ Exercises for Lesson 24

1. How do you say "still" or "not yet" in Korean?

(   )

2. Please write "I do not know yet" in Korean.

(   )

3. "Already" is "벌써". How do you say "Is it already over?/Did it already finish?"

(   )

Check the answers on **p.199**

Remember, although 벌써 and 이미 appear to have the same meaning, native speakers often distinguish the two by using them in different contexts.

4. How do you say "He already graduated from school"?
   - You, and probably the other person, have known this information for a long time.

그 사람은 (   ) 학교를 졸업했어요.

5. How do you say "He already graduated from school"?
   - You may have found out this information just recently, or you already knew about this, but the other person may have not known about it prior to you telling him/her.

그 사람은 (   ) 학교를 졸업했어요!

LESSON 25

Someone, Something, Somewhere, Someday

누군가, 무언가, 어딘가, 언젠가

Track 49

In English, when changing the adverbs "when", "what", "who", or "where" to indefinite words (words with no definite meaning), the words change form and become compound words.

When = Someday

What = Something

Who = Someone

Where = Somewhere

In Korean, it is much easier to create these indefinite words. Just simply add -ㄴ가 to the end
[-(n)-ga]
of the word.

For example :

누구 (who) - **누군가** (someone)
[nu-gu]   [nu-gun-ga]

뭐 (what) - **뭔가** (= **무언가**) (something)
[mwo]   [mwon-ga]   [mu-eon-ga]

어디 (where) - **어딘가** (somewhere)
[eo-di]   [eo-din-ga]

언제 (when) - **언젠가** (someday)
[eon-je]   [eon-jen-ga]

Sample Sentences

언젠가 미국에 가고 싶어요.
[eon-jen-ga mi-gu-ge ga-go si-peo-yo.]
= I want to go to the United States someday.

언제 미국에 가고 싶어요?
[eon-je mi-gu-ge ga-go si-peo-yo?]
= When do you want to go to the United States?

Track 49

언젠가 일본에 갈 거예요.
[eon-jen-ga il-bo-ne gal kkeo-ye-yo.]
= I am going to go to Japan one day.

언제 일본에 갈 거예요?
[eon-je il-bo-ne gal kkeo-ye-yo?]
= When are you going to go to Japan?

뭐 찾았어요?
[mwo cha-ja-sseo-yo?]
= What did you find?

뭔가 찾았어요?
[mwon-ga cha-ja-sseo-yo?]
= Did you find something?

뭔가 이상해요.
[mwon-ga i-sang-hae-yo.]
= Something is strange.

Conjunctions, Tenses,

뭐가 이상해요?
[mwo-ga i-sang-hae-yo?]
= What is strange?

누구 만날 거예요?
[nu-gu man-nal kkeo-ye-yo?]
= Whom will you meet?

누군가 만날 거예요?
[nu-gun-ga man-nal kkeo-ye-yo?]
= Will you meet someone?

누군가 왔어요.
[nu-gun-ga wa-sseo-yo.]
= Someone came.

어디에 있어요?
[eo-di-e i-sseo-yo?]
= Where is it?

Track 49

여기 어딘가에 있어요.
[yeo-gi eo-din-ga-e i-sseo-yo.]
= It is here somewhere.

* However, in Korean, just as in other languages, this usage rule is not always kept by everyone. What does this mean? It means that EVEN when the intended meaning is "someday", 언제 can be used instead of 언젠가. Likewise, 뭐 can be used for "something", 어디 for "somewhere", and 누구 for "someone".

The distinction between 언제 and 언젠가 is stronger than the distinction between other words, but there are many situations in which 언젠가 can be replaced with 언제. When using the original interrogative word rather than -ㄴ가, pay attention to your intonation. The emphasis should be on the verbs, not the actual interrogative word.

Sample Sentences

뭐 샀어요? (stress is on 뭐)
[mwo sa-sseo-yo?]
= What did you buy?

뭐 샀어요? (stress is on 샀어요)

= Did you buy something?

언제 중국에 갈 거예요? (stress is on 언제)
[eon-je jung-gu-ge gal kkeo-ye-yo?]
= When are you going to go to China?

언제 중국에 갈 거예요? (stress is on 갈 거예요?)

= Are you going to go to China someday/one of these days?

Track 49

어디 가요? (stress is on 어디)
[eo-di ga-yo?]
= Where are you going?

어디 가요? (stress is on 가요?)

= Are you going somewhere?

오늘 뭐 배웠어요? (stress is on 배웠어요?)
[o-neul mwo bae-wo-sseo-yo?]
= Did you learn something today?

오늘 뭐 배웠어요? (stress is on 뭐)

= What did you learn today?

Conjunctions, Tenses,

Sample Dialogue

Track 50

A: 여행 좋아해요?
[yeo-haeng jo-a-hae-yo?]

B: 네, 좋아해요. 어딘가로 떠나는 거 좋아해요.
[ne, jo-a-hae-yo. eo-din-ga-ro tteo-na-neun geo jo-a-hae-yo.]

A: 저도 여행 정말 좋아해요. 항상 어딘가로 떠나고 싶어요.
[jeo-do yeo-haeng jeong-mal jo-a-hae-yo. hang-sang eo-din-ga-ro tteo-na-go si-peo-yo.]

A: Do you like traveling?

B: Yes, I do. I like leaving to go somewhere.

A: I also really like traveling. I always want to leave to go somewhere.

🖉 Exercises for Lesson 25

1. If "when" is "언제", how do you say "someday" in Korean?

(   )

2. Since "what" is "뭐", how do you write "something" in Korean?

(   )

3. How do you say "When are you going to go to Japan?"

(   )

4. Please write "I am going to go to Japan one day."

(   )

5. How do you say "Something is strange"?

(   )

Check the answers on **p.199**

Conjunctions, Tenses,

LESSON **26**

Imperative

-(으)세요

Learning to ask or tell someone to do something for you is one of the most essential things to learn in any language. Whether the intention is to be polite or not so polite, learning how to construct imperative sentences in Korean will come handy every single day.

Track 51

To tell someone to do something, add **-(으)세요** to the verb stem.
[-(eu)-se-yo]

> ### *Conjugation*
> Verb stem ending in a consonant + -으세요
> Verb stem ending in a vowel or the consonant ㄹ + -세요

Ex)

시작하다 = to begin, to start
[si-ja-ka-da]

시작하 + -세요 = 시작하세요 = Please begin.
[si-ja-ka-se-yo]

161

오다 = to come
[o-da]
오 + -세요 = 오세요 = Please come.
[o-se-yo]

쉬다 = to rest
[swi-da]
쉬 + -세요 = 쉬세요 = Please get some rest.
[swi-se-yo]

고르다 = to choose, to pick
[go-reu-da]
고르 + -세요 = 고르세요 = Please choose.
[go-reu-se-yo]

접다 = to fold
[jeop-tta]
접 + -으세요 = 접으세요 = Please fold it.
[jeo-beu-se-yo]

Exception:

When a verb stem ends with the consonant ㄹ, drop the ㄹ and add -세요.

팔다 = to sell
[pal-da]
팔 → 파 + 세요 = 파세요 = Please sell it.
[pa-se-yo]

The focus of this lesson is presenting -(으)세요 as a way to tell someone to do something. The honorific suffix -시 is included in this ending, and there are a couple variations of this depending on the type of language (honorific, informal), but please remember that this ending is considered "formal" or "polite".

Sample Sentences

내일 세 시에 오세요.
[nae-il se si-e o-se-yo.]
= Please come here at three o'clock tomorrow.

162

공부하세요!
[gong-bu-ha-se-yo!]
= Study! Do your studies!

경은 씨, 빨리 일하세요.
[gyeong-eun ssi, ppal-li i-ra-se-yo.]
= Kyeong-eun, hurry up and get some work done!

경은 씨, 쉬세요.
[gyeong-eun ssi, swi-se-yo.]
= Kyeong-eun, please get some rest.

이거 저한테 파세요.
[i-geo jeo-han-te pa-se-yo.]
= Please sell this to me.

조심하세요.
[jo-si-ma-se-yo.]
= Be careful!

Track 51

Some fixed expressions using -세요:

When going into a store or restaurant, an employee will most often say:

1. 어서 오세요.
  [eo-seo o-se-yo.]
= (lit. Come quickly) Welcome.

When a person is leaving and you are staying:

2. 안녕히 가세요.
[an-nyeong-hi ga-se-yo.]
= (lit. Go peacefully) Goodbye.

If you are leaving, and the other person is staying:

3. 안녕히 계세요.
[an-nyeong-hi gye-se-yo.]
= (lit. Stay peacefully) Goodbye.

How to say "Goodnight" in Korean:

4. 안녕히 주무세요.
[an-nyeong-hi ju-mu-se-yo.]
= (lit. Sleep peacefully) Goodnight.

Some words change their forms specifically for polite/formal language, but those will be

covered in a future lesson.

Track 51

Conjunctions, Tenses,

Sample Dialogue

**Track
52**

A: 서점에서 TTMIK 책 사 오세요.
[seo-jeo-me-seo TTMIK chaek sa o-se-yo.]

B: 만약에 없으면요?
[ma-nya-ge eop-sseu-myeon-nyo?]

A: 없으면 그냥 오세요.
[eop-sseu-myeon geu-nyang o-se-yo.]

A: Please buy me a TTMIK book from the
bookstore.

B: What if they don't have one?

A: If so, just come back (here).

✏️ Exercises for Lesson **26**

Check the answers on **p.199**

1. When you want to tell or ask someone to do something, you add the ending -(으)세요 to the verb stem. How would you say "Do it"?

(   )

2. "To rest" is "쉬다". How do you say "Get some rest"?

(   )

3. "To be careful" is "조심하다". How do you write "Be careful!"?
[jo-si-ma-da]

(   )

4. "To study" is "공부하다" and "doing something difficult" is described in Korean as doing it
[gong-bu-ha-da]
"열심히". How do you say "Study hard!"?
[yeol-ssi-mi]

(   )

5. When you go into a shop or a restaurant, what will the people who are working there say to you to mean "Welcome"?

(   )

LESSON 27

Please do it for me

-아/어/여 주세요

Track
53

In the previous lesson, you learned how to tell someone to do something using -(으)세요.
[-(eu)-se-yo]
Although this is perfectly acceptable, there is an even more polite way to ask the same
question.

Rather than adding -(으)세요 after a verb stem, add **-아/어/여 + 주세요**. By adding this
[-a/eo/yeo]   [ju-se-yo]
verb ending, the sentence has a much nicer tone and has a nuance of asking someone for a
favor or asking the other person to do something "for you".

Ex)

오다 = to come
[o-da]
오세요. = Please come.
[o-se-yo.]
와 주세요. = Please do me a favor and come.
[wa ju-se-yo.]

하다 = to do
[ha-da]
하세요. = Do it.
[ha-se-yo.]

167

해 주세요. = Please do me a favor and do it for me.
[hae ju-se-yo.]

Using -아/어/여 주세요 rather than just -(으)세요 not only makes the sentence more polite, but it also adds the meaning of "please do it for me". There is no need to say the phrase "저를 위해서", which literally means "for me" if -아/어/여 주세요 is used.
[jeo-reul wi-hae-seo]

For example, "아이스크림 사세요" can mean "buy yourself some ice cream", "buy ice cream
[a-i-seu-keu-rim sa-se-yo]
for your friends", or simply just "buy some ice cream". On the other hand, using -아/어/여 주세요 to say "아이스크림 사 주세요" means "please buy ME some ice cream". If someone
[a-i-seu-keu-rim sa ju-se-yo]
selling ice cream says this, the meaning is "please buy ice cream from me if you want to help me".

Track 53

When asking for help, often at times, it is more natural to add -아/어/여 주세요. For example, it is not very natural to say "저를 도우세요!" (돕다 = to help) when the intended
[jeo-reul do-u-se-yo!]   [dop-tta]
meaning is "help me!" To sound more natural and a bit more polite, say "저를 도와 주세요"
[jeo-reul do-wa ju-se-yo]
or just "도와 주세요".

Take a look at the difference of meaning between -(으)세요 and -아/어/여 주세요.

가르치다 = to teach
[ga-reu-chi-da]
가르치세요. = Teach. / Please teach. (to whom is unknown)
[ga-reu-chi-se-yo.]
가르쳐 주세요. = Please teach me.
[ga-reu-cheo ju-se-yo.]
경은 씨한테 가르쳐 주세요. = Please teach Kyeong-eun (how to do that).
[gyeong-eun ssi-han-te ga-reu-cheo ju-se-yo.]
경은 씨한테 스페인어 가르쳐 주세요. = Please teach Kyeong-eun Spanish.
[gyeong-eun ssi-han-te seu-pe-i-neo ga-reu-cheo ju-se-yo.]
스페인어 가르쳐 주세요. = Please teach me Spanish.
[seu-pe-i-neo ga-reu-cheo ju-se-yo.]

보다 = to see
[bo-da]

보세요. = See it. / Please see it.
[bo-se-yo.]

봐 주세요. = Please see it, and I would appreciate it. / Please be kind and see it.
[bwa ju-se-yo.]

이거 봐 주세요. = Please look at this.
[i-geo bwa ju-se-yo.]

숙제 봐 주세요. = Please look at my homework.
[suk-jje bwa ju-se-yo.]

주세요 is derived from 주다, which means "to give". By adding 주세요 after a verb, the meaning of "do it for me, please" is also added. As for -아/어/여, think of it as a "helper" to make the pronunciation a bit easier.

To speak a little less formally, say 줘요 rather than 주세요. It is more casual than 주세요 but more polite than just -세요.

Track 53

Sample Sentences

영어를 배우고 있어요. 도와주세요.
[yeong-eo-reul bae-u-go i-sseo-yo. do-wa-ju-se-yo.]
= I am learning English. Please help me.

도와줄 수 있어요?
[do-wa-jul ssu i-sseo-yo?]
= Can you help me?

배고파요. 김밥 사 주세요.
[bae-go-pa-yo. gim-ppap sa ju-se-yo.]
= I am hungry. Buy me some gimbap.

무서워요. 같이 가 주세요.
[mu-seo-wo-yo. ga-chi ga ju-se-yo.]
= I am scared. Please go with me.

Sample Dialogue

A: 석진 씨, 잠깐 이야기할 수 있어요?
[seok-jjin ssi, jam-kkan i-ya-gi-hal ssu i-sseo-yo?]

B: 아... 지금요?
[a... ji-geu-myo?]

A: 지금 바쁘면 3시까지 1층으로
와 주세요.
[ji-geum ba-ppeu-myeon se-si-kka-ji il-cheung-eu-ro
wa ju-se-yo.]

B: 네, 알겠습니다.
[ne, al-get-sseum-ni-da.]

A: Seokjin, can we talk for a moment?

B: Ah... now?

A: If you are busy now, please come
down to the first floor by 3 o'clock.

B: Okay, I will.

✏ *Exercises for Lesson 27*

1. The expression that makes a sentence translate to "for me" or "do it for me" is -아/어/여 주세요. How do you say "Do this for me, please"?

( )

2. The verb "to teach" is "가르치다". How do you say "Please teach me English"?

( )

3. The verb "to buy" is "사다". How do you say "Please buy me that over there"?
[sa-da]

( )

4. How do you say "Please have a look at this"?

( )

5. "Can you come with me?" is "같이 갈 수 있어요?". How do you add the nuance of "Can you do
[ga-chi gal ssu i-sseo-yo?]
me a favor and come with me?" to the sentence?

( )

Check the answers on **p.199**

171

LESSON **28**

Method, Way

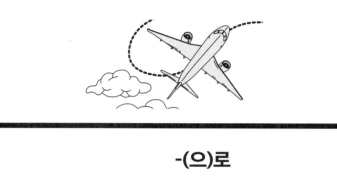

-(으)로

Track 55

You have already learned a handful of Korean particles and how to use them through the previous lessons in this book. Get ready to add a new one to the bunch! Learn the meaning and usage of -(으)로 with this lesson.
[-(eu)-ro]

> ### *Conjugation*
>
> Nouns ending with a consonant + -으로
>
> Nouns ending in a vowel or the consonant "ㄹ" + -로

-(으)로 connects a noun and a verb very closely and can have various functions. -(으)로 can mark the ingredients an object is made of, the cause of a disease or something that happened, the direction in which someone is going, or the status or identity of a person doing something. Take a look at some examples:

Conjunctions, Tenses,

Ex)

(1) 나무로 만들다
[na-mu-ro man-deul-da]
= 나무 (wood) + -로 + 만들다 (to make)

= to make (something) with wood

Someone made this table with wood. = 누가 이 테이블을 나무로 만들었어요.
[nu-ga i te-i-beu-reul na-mu-ro man-deu-reo-sseo-yo.]

(2) 왼쪽으로 가다
[oen-jjo-geu-ro ga-da]
= 왼쪽 (left side) + -으로 + 가다 (to go)

= to go to the left

= to go through the left side

(3) 이 길로 가다
[i gil-lo ga-da]
= 이 (this) 길 (street / road) + -로 + 가다 (to go)

= to go down this path

= to go down this road

🎤

Track 55

(4) 펜으로 쓰다
[pe-neu-ro sseu-da]
= 펜 (pen) + -으로 + 쓰다 (to write)

= to write with a pen

(5) 한국어로 말하다
[han-gu-geo-ro ma-ra-da]
= 한국어 (Korean) + 로 + 말하다 (to speak / to talk)

= to speak in Korean

(6) 치즈로 유명하다
[chi-jeu-ro yu-myeong-ha-da]
= 치즈 (cheese) + 로 + 유명하다 (to be famous)

= to be famous for cheese

(7) 사고로 다치다
[sa-go-ro da-chi-da]

= 사고 (accident) + 로 + 다치다 (to get hurt)

= to get hurt in (from) an accident

There is a common factor in the way -(으)로 was used in the previous sentences. Can you identify it?

By using -(으)로, something is used as a channel, tool, device, or a method.

Sample Sentences

Track 55

이거 뭐로 만들었어요?
[i-geo mwo-ro man-deu-reo-sseo-yo?]
= What did you make this with?

= What is this made of?

오늘 택시로 왔어요?
[o-neul taek-ssi-ro wa-sseo-yo?]
= Did you come by taxi today?

버스로 갈 거예요.
[beo-sseu-ro gal kkeo-ye-yo.]
= I am going to go by bus.

저를 친구로 생각해요?
[jeo-reul chin-gu-ro saeng-ga-kae-yo?]
= Do you think of me as a friend?

2번 출구로 나오세요.
[i-beon chul-gu-ro na-o-se-yo.]
= Come out through exit number 2.

저는 Talk To Me In Korean으로 한국어 공부해요.
[jeo-neun Talk To Me In Korean-eu-ro han-gu-geo gong-bu-hae-yo.]
= I study Korean through Talk To Me In Korean.

Track 55

Telling Time, and More

Sample Dialogue

A: 2월에 캐나다로 돌아가요?
[i-wo-re kae-na-da-ro do-ra-ga-yo?]

B: 네. 그런데 다시 올 거예요.
[ne. geu-reon-de da-si ol kkeo-ye-yo.]

A: 언제요?
[eon-je-yo?]

B: 여름에요.
[yeo-reu-me-yo.]

A: Are you going back to Canada in February?

B: Yes, but I will come here again.

A: When?

B: In the summer.

Conjunctions, Tenses,

✏ *Exercises for Lesson 28*

1. The word that indicates a method in which, or an ingredient with which, an object is made is "-으로" or "-로". When do you use "-으로" instead of "-로"?

(   )

2. How do you say "with a pen"?

(   )

3. The word for "a chair" is "의자"[ui-ja], and the word for "wood" is "나무"[na-mu]. Please write "They made this chair out of wood."

(   )

4. How do you say "Please speak in Korean for me"?

(   )

5. Please write "What did you make this with?"

(   )

Check the answers on **p.199**

LESSON **29**

All, More

다, 더

Track 57

With this lesson, you will learn the Korean words for "all" and "more" as well as how to apply these words to Korean sentences to sound more natural.

다 = all, entirely, whole

더 = more

For many sentences in English where a speaker would use adjectives and nouns, Korean speakers use adverbs and verbs. This often becomes a challenge when translating, as things do not quite translate directly, but having this knowledge as a learner of Korean will ultimately lead to more natural-sounding Korean.

Take a look at how 다 is used:
[da]

Ex)

(1) 다 주세요.
[da ju-se-yo.]
= Give me all of it.

(2) 우유 다 주세요.
[u-yu da ju-se-yo.]
= Give me all the milk.

(3) 다 했어요.
[da hae-sseo-yo.]
= I have done all of it.

(4) 다 왔어요?
[da wa-sseo-yo?]
= Are we there yet? (lit. Did we all come? / Did we come to all of it?)

= Did everyone come?

Track 57

(5) 다 살 거예요?
[da sal kkeo-ye-yo?]
= Are you going to buy all of it?

In some of the examples above, it looks as if the word 다 is working as a noun, and it is, but it has a stronger influence on the verbs and acts as more of an adverb.

커피를 마시다
[keo-pi-reul ma-si-da]
= to drink coffee

커피를 다 마시다
= to drink all the coffee

179

In the second sentence previously, the English word "all" was used to describe "the coffee", but in Korean, the word 다 was used to describe the action of drinking (마시다).

책을 읽다
[chae-geul ik-tta]
= to read a book

책을 다 읽다
[chae-geul da ik-tta]
= to read all of the book
= to finish reading the book

Track 57

> Q : Then how do you say "all of the book" or "the entire book", if the word 다 only modifies verbs?
>
> A : You can use other words like 전체 or 전부. "The entire book" is 책 전체 or 책 전부, but
> [jeon-che]   [jeon-bu]
> this might not sound very natural when used out of proper context. In most cases, it is better to use 다.

Let's look at how 더 is used.
[deo]

Ex)

(1) 더 주세요.
[deo ju-se-yo.]
= Please give me more.

(2) 더 있어요.
[deo i-sseo-yo.]
= There is more.

180

(3) 더 사고 싶어요.
[deo sa-go si-peo-yo.]
= I want to buy more.

(4) 옷 더 사고 싶어요.
[ot deo sa-go si-peo-yo.]
= I want to buy more clothes.

(5) 뭐가 더 좋아요?
[mwo-ga deo jo-a-yo?]
= Which is better?

The explanation for 다 also applies to the word 더, especially when modifying verbs. It may look as if 더 is used as a noun in sentences (3) and (4), but, it is not! When saying "더 사고 싶어요" or "옷 더 사고 싶어요", the meaning is closer to "I want to do the 'action of buying' more" rather than "I want to buy more" or "I want to buy more clothes".

Track
57

10분 기다려 주세요.

= Please wait for 10 minutes.

10분 더 기다려 주세요.
[sip-ppun deo gi-da-ryeo ju-se-yo.]
= Please wait for 10 more minutes.

In English, the phrase is said as "10 more minutes", but in Korean, it literally translates to "do the action of waiting for 10 minutes + more".

181

Sample Sentences

전화 다 했어요?
[jeo-nwa da hae-sseo-yo?]
= Did you finish talking on the phone?

= Did you make all the phone calls?

= Did everyone make a phone call?

준비 다 했어요.
[jun-bi da hae-sseo-yo.]
= I did all the preparation.

= I prepared everything.

= I finished the preparation.

= All of us are prepared.

Track 57

더 보여 주세요.
[deo bo-yeo ju-se-yo.]
= Show me more.

= Show me more of it.

더 공부하고 싶으면, TTMIK에 오세요.
[deo gong-bu-ha-go si-peu-myeon TTMIK-e o-se-yo.]
= If you want to study more, come to TTMIK.

= If you want to do more studying, come to TTMIK.

Sample Dialogue

Track 58

A: 한국어를 더 잘하고 싶어요.
[han-gu-geo-reul deo ja-ra-go si-peo-yo.]

B: 지금도 잘해요.
[ji-geum-do ja-rae-yo.]

A: 아니에요.
[a-ni-e-yo.]

B: 그럼 더 열심히 하세요.
[geu-reom deo yeol-ssi-mi ha-se-yo.]

A: I want to be better at Korean.

B: You are already good at it.

A: No, I am not.

B: Then study harder.

✏️ Exercises for Lesson 29

Check the answers on p.199

1. What is the word for "more" in Korean?

(   )

2. What is the word for "all" in Korean?

(   )

3. How do you say "Did you do all of it?" or "Did you finish doing it?"

(   )

4. How do you say "I did all my homework"?

(   )

5. Please write "I want to buy more" in Korean.

(   )

6. How do you say "I want to buy all"?

(   )

Conjunctions, Tenses,

LESSON **30**

Don't do it

-지 마세요

You have already learned how to tell or ask someone to do something for you, but how do you tell someone to "stop doing" something or "do not do" something?

Track
59

Use the following verb + -(으)세요:
[-(eu)-se-yo]

말다 = to quit doing; to not do; to stop doing
[mal-da]

When using -(으)세요 with this word, it becomes 마세요. When combining 마세요 with
[ma-se-yo]
other verbs to say "do not do" or "stop doing" something, the suffix -지 is needed after the
[-ji]
verb stem.

> ### Conjugation
> Verb stem + -지 마세요

Ex)

가지 마세요. = Don't go.
[ga-ji ma-se-yo.]
아직 가지 마세요. = Don't go yet.
[a-jik ga-ji ma-se-yo.]
하지 마세요. = Don't do it. / Drop it. / Stop it. / Forget about it.
[ha-ji ma-se-yo.]
사지 마세요. = Don't buy it.
[sa-ji ma-se-yo.]

Sample Sentences.

만지지 마세요.
[man-ji-ji ma-se-yo.]
= Don't touch it.

웃지 마세요.
[ut-jji ma-se-yo.]
= Don't laugh.

Track 59

걱정하지 마세요.
[geok-jjeong-ha-ji ma-se-yo.]
= Don't worry.

경은 씨한테 말하지 마세요.
[gyeong-eun ssi-han-te ma-ra-ji ma-se-yo.]
= Please don't tell Kyeong-eun (about it).

아직 보내지 마세요. 아직 다 안 썼어요.
[a-jik bo-nae-ji ma-se-yo. a-jik da an sseo-sseo-yo.]
= Don't send it yet. I have not finished writing it.

Sample Dialogue

Track
60

A: 내일 아침에 강남역으로 오는 거 잊지 마세요.
[nae-il a-chi-me gang-nam-nyeo-geu-ro o-neun geo it-jji ma-se-yo.]

B: 네. 몇 시까지 가요?
[ne. myeot si-kka-ji ga-yo?]

A: 9시까지 오세요.
[a-hop-ssi-kka-ji o-se-yo.]

A: Don't forget to come to Gangnam Station tomorrow morning.

B: Okay. What time should I be there?

A: Please come by 9 o'clock.

Telling Time, and More

✏️ Exercises for Lesson 30

1. The Korean word for "to quit doing/to not do/ to stop doing" is "말다". How do you say "Don't do it"?

(   )

2. "To buy" is "사다". Please write "Don't buy it."
[sa-da]

(   )

3. The word for "not yet" or "yet" is "아직". How do you say "Don't do it yet"?

(   )

4. The word for "to give up" is "포기하다". Please write "Don't give up."
[po-gi-ha-da]

(   )

5. "A lot" is "많이" and "too much" is "너무 많이". How do you say "Don't buy too much of it"?
[ma-ni]   [neo-mu ma-ni]

(   )

Check the answers on **p.199**

T-MONEY
(티머니 카드)

T-money is quite possibly the greatest invention to ever grace the streets of Seoul and surrounding Gyeonggi-do, and it'll be the best investment of your life to get one of these to carry around with you when you come here. T-money comes in all shapes and sizes, is rechargeable, and is useful in every means of public transportation that Seoul and Gyeonggi-do has to offer (hence the name "T-money").

So let's say that you've arrived in Korea and don't have T-money yet. How do you get it?

Luckily, you can purchase and re-fill T-money at all subway ticket booths. These automated machines are pretty nifty. You can also purchase and recharge T-money at almost every convenience store in Seoul. Most stores have a T-money logo in the window so you know for sure that you can purchase and re-charge there. There are even a few convenience stores at Incheon Airport on the arrival floor where you can do this, so when you get to

Seoul or Gyeonggi-do, you'll already have it. This saves you from being super awkward and basically wearing a sign on your forehead that says "I'm a tourist!" when you try to take a bus ride by paying with cash. Actually, it's not THAT awkward to pay with cash, but why pay with cash when you can get a discount by paying with T-money?!

Discount? Yeah, that's right! Everyone loves discounts, and T-money gives you 100W off the basic cash fare, which is essentially 1,150W for every 10km traveled. Since transportation cost in Seoul is figured by distance, having a T-money card will provide you with a discount on up to 4 transfers on the subways and buses when you need to.

You can get a regular T-money card for 3,000W, and other speciality cards, key chains, phone charms, etc. range from 6,000W to 15,000W. Different cards are sold at different locations, so check out this link to see all the different kinds of T-money cards and where they're sold: http://t-zone.co.kr/

T-money is also refundable, but you have to pay a 500W fee. If your balance is under 20,000W, just take your T-money to a GS25, 7-11, Buy the Way, MiniStop, HomePlus 365, or GS Watsons store to receive the refund on the balance only. If your balance is up to or less than 30,000W, you may only receive a refund at CU convenience stores. If your balance is up to or less than 50,000W, take your card to the T-money Service Desk on any Seoul subway

line at a number of stations in Seoul to get your money back (it may be difficult to find a T-money Service Desk outside the Seoul Metropolitan Area). Or, you can just keep the

T-money card and the money on it for the next time you come to Korea because it NEVER expires!!

If you won't be in Seoul for an extended amount of time and don't want to purchase a T-money card, another option is the M-Pass card or the Seoul City Pass Plus. With the M-Pass card, also known as Metropolitan Pass, you can ride the Seoul Subway Lines 1-9, the standard AREX (Incheon Airport Rail Express), standard trains (not express), metro trains (except the Shinbundang Line) and Seoul buses (except red buses). You can take advantage of these great modes of transportation up to 20 times per day without a limit on distance. The M-pass has a T-money function and can be used in taxis and when making convenience store purchases even if you have used it 20 times on the aforementioned public transportation methods. Passes are valid for the designated time period and expire at midnight on the last day.

There are five different types of M-passes: 1-day, 2-day, 3-day, 5-day, and 7-day which are available for purchase at Seoul Travel Information Centers (I-Tour Centers) in the Passenger Terminal at Incheon Airport. When purchasing an M-pass, you must pay a completely refundable deposit of 4,500 won in addition to a non-refundable service charge of 500 won. The refundable deposit will be returned to you in addition to any remaining T-money balance when you return the pass at any of the Seoul Travel Information Centers.

M-Pass Prices

1-day = 10,000W
2-days= 18,000W
3-days= 25,500W
5-day = 42,500W

7-day = 59,500W

The Seoul City Pass Plus Card is a pretty flippin' sweet deal if you're a tourist and plan to be in Seoul for a while. It's essentially a T-money card with added benefits designed for tourists. You can ride any bus or subway in Seoul until you run out of money and have to re-fill just like a regular T-money card, but you also have the ability to use the card at any of the four royal palaces in Seoul as well as for

most convenience store purchases. The benefits don't stop there! You can take any of the Seoul City Tour Bus routes at a 5% discount, too! With your Seoul City Pass Plus card, you also receive a booklet and discount coupons to use everywhere in Seoul. This pass also gets you discounts at 60+ participating stores that include restaurants, attractions, beauty stores, and many more! You get all of this great stuff for only 500W more than a regular T-money card. Um, yeah...totally awesome!

You can purchase and recharge the Seoul City Pass Plus Card at any GS25, CU, Mini Stop, Buy The Way, or 7-11 convenience stores in Korea. You can also recharge at any automatic subway ticket booth. This card is also refundable, but there is a 500W convenience fee to get your money back.

Now that you know how to get around Seoul with a few different payment options, we hope to see you here soon!

Before you close this book,
we want to say "congratulations" for finishing
TTMIK Level 2!
Way to go, and we'll see you in Level 3!

ANSWERS

for Level 2, Lessons 1 ~ 30

Answers for Level 2, Lesson 1

1. 청바지 입을 거예요.
[cheong-ba-ji i-beul kkeo-ye-yo.]
2. 뭐 팔 거예요?
[mwo pal kkeo-ye-yo?]
3. 누구 만날 거예요?
[nu-gu man-nal kkeo-ye-yo?]
4. 언제 점심 먹을 거예요? or
[eon-je jeom-sim meo-geul kkeo-ye-yo?]
   점심 언제 먹을 거예요?
[jeom-sim eon-je meo-geul kkeo-ye-yo?]
5. 내일 뭐 할 거예요?
[nae-il mwo hal kkeo-ye-yo?]

Answers for Level 2, Lesson 2

1. 를

2. 을

3. 를

4. 를

5. 을

Answers for Level 2, Lesson 3

1. 그리고

2. 그래서

3. 그래서

4. 그리고

5. 그리고

Answers for Level 2, Lesson 4

1. 랑 / 하고

2. 랑 / 하고

3. 이랑 / 하고

4. 이랑 / 하고

5. 랑 / 하고

Answers for Level 2, Lesson 5

1. 일요일 = b. Sunday

2. 화요일 = g. Tuesday

3. 토요일 = a. Saturday

4. 목요일 = c. Thursday

5. 수요일 = f. Wednesday

6. 월요일 = d. Monday

7. 금요일 = e. Friday

Answers for Level 2, Lesson 6

1. 그렇지만 / 그런데

2. 피곤해요. 그렇지만 / 그런데 영화 보고 싶어요.

3. 좋아요. 그렇지만 / 그런데 비싸요.
[jo-a-yo]   [bi-ssa-yo.]
4. 어제는 비 왔어요. 그렇지만 /
[eo-je-neun bi wa-sseo-yo.]
   그런데 지금은 비 안 와요.
[ji-geu-meun bi an wa-yo.]
5. 어제 학교에 갔어요. 그렇지만 /

   그런데 일요일이었어요.

Answers for Level 2, Lesson 7

1. 친구한테 / 친구한테서 받았어요.
[chin-gu-han-te / chin-gu-han-te-seo ba-da-sseo-yo.]
2. 누구한테 물어봤어요?
[nu-gu-han-te mu-reo-bwa-sseo-yo?]
3. 저한테 질문 있어요?
[jeo-han-te jil-mun i-sseo-yo?]
4. 동생한테 이거 줄 거예요. or
[dong-saeng-han-te i-geo jul kkeo-ye-yo.]
   이거 동생한테 줄 거예요.
[i-geo dong-saeng-han-te jul kkeo-ye-yo.]
5. 친구한테 / 친구한테서 이거 얻었어요. or
[chin-gu-han-te/chin-gu-han-te-seo i-geo eo-deo-sseo-yo.]
   이거 친구한테 / 친구한테서 얻었어요.
[i-geo chin-gu-han-te/chin-gu-han-te-seo eo-deo-sseo-yo.]

Answers for Level 2, Lesson 8

1. 몇 시예요?

2. 세 시

3. 한 시 십오 분

4. 다섯 시 사십칠 분
   [sa-sip-chil bun]
5. 열 시 삼십 분 or 열 시 반

Answers for Level 2, Lesson 9

1. 세 개

2. 다섯 명

3. 의자 세 개

4. 몇 명 있어요? or 몇 사람 있어요?

5. 두 명 있어요. or 두 사람 있어요.

Answers for Level 2, Lesson 10

1. 책 읽고 있어요.
   [chaek il-kko i-sseo-yo.]
2. 뭐 하고 있어요?

3. 뭐 하고 있었어요?

4. 자고 있었어요.
   [ja-go i-sseo-sseo-yo.]
5. 공부하고 있을 거예요.

Answers for Level 2, Lesson 11

1. 저는 학생이에요.

2. 제 이름은 민수예요.
   [min-su-ye-yo.]
3. 저는 20살이에요.
   [seu-mu-sa-ri-e-yo.]
4. 저는 서울에 살아요.

5. 반갑습니다.

Answers for Level 2, Lesson 12

1. 9월

2. 일

3. 9월 25일
   [gu-wol i-si-bo-il]
4. 몇 월

5. 며칠

6. 생일이 몇 월 며칠이에요?

Answers for Level 2, Lesson 13

1. 저도 선생님이에요.
   [jeo-do]
2. 한국어도 공부해요?
   [han-gu-geo-do]
3. 오늘도 일해요?
   [o-neul-do]
4. 물도 있어요.
   [mul-do]
5. 저도 이것 주세요. / 저 이것도 주세요.
   [jeo-do i-geot ju-se-yo.] [jeo i-geot-tto ju-se-yo.]

Answers for Level 2, Lesson 14

1. 보기도 하다

2. 팔기도 하다

3. 저는 영어를 가르쳐요.

4. 저는 영어를 가르치기도 해요.

5. 저는 수학을 가르치기도 해요.
   [jeo-neun su-ha-geul ga-reu-chi-gi-do hae-yo.]

Answers for Level 2, Lesson 15

1. 만

2. 이것만

3. 보기만 하다

4. 커피만 마셔요.
   [keo-pi-man ma-syeo-yo.]

5. 책 한 권만 주문했어요.

Answers for Level 2, Lesson 16

1. 조금 비싸요.

2. 아주 재미있어요.
[a-ju jae-mi-i-sseo-yo.]

3. 정말 이상해요.

4. 별로 안 비싸요.

5. 전혀 재미없어요.

Answers for Level 2, Lesson 17

1. 갈 수 있어요.
[gal su i-sseo-yo.]

2. 할 수 없어요. / 못 해요.
[hal su eop-sseo-yo.] [mot hae-yo.]

3. 이거 할 수 있어요?
[i-geo hal su i-sseo-yo?]

4. 지금 만날 수 있어요?
[ji-geum man-nal su i-sseo-yo?]

5. 수영할 수 있어요?
[su-yeong-hal su i-sseo-yo?]

Answers for Level 2, Lesson 18

1. -을/를 잘하다

2. -을/를 못하다

3. 못 하다

4. 저는 수영을 잘해요.

5. 저는 노래를 잘 못 해요.

Answers for Level 2, Lesson 19

1. 먹는 것

2. 가는 것

3. 책 읽는 것 좋아해요.
[chaek ing-neun geot jo-a-hae-yo.]

4. 매운 것 안 좋아해요.
[mae-un geot an jo-a-hae-yo.]

5. 제 취미는 영화 보는 거예요.

Answers for Level 2, Lesson 20

1. Using 되다 is more common in colloquial situations.

2. 가야 돼요. / 가야 해요.
[ga-ya dwae-yo.] [ga-ya hae-yo.]

3. 써야 돼요. / 써야 해요.
[sseo-ya dwae-yo.] [sseo-ya hae-yo.]

4. 지금 해야 돼요. / 지금 해야 해요.
[ji-geum hae-ya dwae-yo.]

5. 내일 어디 가야 돼요? / 내일 어디 가야 해요?
[nae-il eo-di ga-ya dwae-yo?]

Answers for Level 2, Lesson 21

1. 더 빠르다

2. 더 좋다

3. 커피는 물보다 더 비싸요.
[keo-pi-neun mul-bo-da deo bi-ssa-yo.]

4. 이 책은 저 책보다 더 재미있어요.
[i chae-geun jeo chaek-ppo-da deo jae-mi-i-sseo-yo.]

5. (저는) 어제보다 더 일찍 왔어요.
[(jeo-neun) eo-je-bo-da deo il-jjik wa-sseo-yo.]

Answers for Level 2, Lesson 22

1. 좋아하다

2. 한국어 좋아요.

3. 한국어를 좋아해요. or 한국어 좋아해요.

4. 민수 씨는 우유를 좋아해요.
[min-su ssi-neun u-yu-reul jo-a-hae-yo.]

5. 뭐가 제일 좋아요?

Answers for Level 2, Lesson 23

1. 만약 지금 자면

2. 보다 = c. to watch

3. 보면 = b. if you watch it, if I watch it

4. 봤으면 = d. if I watched it, if they watched it

5. 볼 거면 = a.if you are going to watch it

6. 내일 비가 오면, 집에 있을 거예요.

Answers for Level 2, Lesson 24

1. 아직

2. 아직 몰라요.

3. 벌써 끝났어요?

4. 이미

그 사람은 이미 학교를 졸업했어요.

5. 벌써

그 사람은 벌써 학교를 졸업했어요!

Answers for Level 2, Lesson 25

1. 언젠가

2. 뭔가

3. 언제 일본에 갈 거예요?

4. 언젠가 일본에 갈 거예요.

5. 뭔가 이상해요.

Level 2 Lesson 26

1. 하세요
[ha-se-yo]

2. 쉬세요

3. 조심하세요!

4. 열심히 공부하세요!

5. 어서오세요. (lit. Come quickly)

Level 2 Lesson 27

1. 이거 해 주세요.

2. 영어 가르쳐 주세요.

3. 저거 사 주세요.
[jeo-geo sa ju-se-yo.]

4. 이거 봐 주세요.
[i-geo bwa ju-se-yo.]

5. 같이 가 줄 수 있어요?
[ga-chi ga jul su i-sseo-yo?]

Level 2 Lesson 28

1. after the nouns ending with a consonant

2. 펜으로

3. 이 의자는 나무로 만들었어요.
[i ui-ja-neun na-mu-ro man-deu-reo-sseo-yo.]

4. 한국어로 말해 주세요.
[han-gu-geo-ro ma-rae ju-se-yo.]

5. 이거 뭐로 만들었어요?

Level 2 Lesson 29

1. 더

2. 다

3. 다 했어요?

4. 숙제를 다 했어요.
[suk-jje-reul da hae-sseo-yo.]

5. 더 사고 싶어요.

6. 다 사고 싶어요.

Level 2 Lesson 30

1. 하지 마세요.

2. 사지 마세요.

3. 아직 하지 마세요.

4. 포기하지 마세요.
[po-gi-ha-ji ma-se-yo.]

5. 너무 많이 사지 마세요.

Notes On Using This Book

Romanization
In each lesson, words and expressions are romanized the first time they appear only. Readers are encouraged not to rely on romanization.

Colored Text
Colored text indicates that there is an accompanying audio file. You can download the MP3 audio files at **https://talktomeinkorean.com/audio**.

Hyphen
Some grammar points have a hyphen attached at the beginning, such as -이/가, -(으)ㄹ 거예요, -(으)려고 하다, and -은/는커녕. This means that the grammar point is dependent, so it needs to be attached to another word such as a noun, a verb, or a particle.

Parentheses
When a grammar point includes parentheses, such as -(으)ㄹ 거예요 or (이)랑, this means that the part in the parentheses can be omitted depending on the word it is attached to.

Slash
When a grammar point has a slash, such as -아/어/여서 or -은/는커녕, this means that only one of the syllables before or after the slash can be used at a time. In other words, -은/는커녕 is used as either -은커녕 or -는커녕, depending on the word it is attached to.

Descriptive Verb
In TTMIK lessons, adjectives in English are referred to as "descriptive verbs" because they can be conjugated as verbs depending on the tense.